T0334093

Cambridge Elements ≡

Elements in the Problems of God
edited by
Michael L. Peterson
Asbury Theological Seminary

GOD AND THE PROBLEM OF LOGIC

Andrew Dennis Bassford
University of Texas at Austin

CAMBRIDGE
UNIVERSITY PRESS

Shaftesbury Road, Cambridge CB2 8EA, United Kingdom

One Liberty Plaza, 20th Floor, New York, NY 10006, USA

477 Williamstown Road, Port Melbourne, VIC 3207, Australia

314–321, 3rd Floor, Plot 3, Splendor Forum, Jasola District Centre, New Delhi – 110025, India

103 Penang Road, #05–06/07, Visioncrest Commercial, Singapore 238467

Cambridge University Press is part of Cambridge University Press & Assessment, a department of the University of Cambridge.

We share the University's mission to contribute to society through the pursuit of education, learning and research at the highest international levels of excellence.

www.cambridge.org
Information on this title: www.cambridge.org/9781009272407

DOI: 10.1017/9781009272391

First published 2023

A catalogue record for this publication is available from the British Library.

ISBN 978-1-009-27240-7 Paperback
ISSN 2754-8724 (online)
ISSN 2754-8716 (print)

God and the Problem of Logic

Elements in the Problems of God

DOI: 10.1017/9781009272391
First published online: May 2023

Andrew Dennis Bassford
University of Texas at Austin

Author for correspondence: Andrew Dennis Bassford, a.d.bassford@utexas.edu

Abstract: Classical theists hold that God is omnipotent. But now suppose a critical atheologian were to ask: Can God create a stone so heavy that even he cannot lift it? This is the dilemma of the stone paradox. God either can or cannot create such a stone. Suppose that God can create it. Then there's something he cannot do – namely, lift the stone. Suppose that God cannot create the stone. Then, again, there's something he cannot do – namely, create it. Either way, God cannot be omnipotent. Among the variety of known theological paradoxes, the paradox of the stone is especially troubling because of its logical purity. It purports to show that one cannot believe in both God and the laws of logic. In the face of the stone paradox, how should the contemporary analytic theist respond? Ought they to revise their belief in theology or their belief in logic? Ought they to lose their religion or lose their mind?

Keywords: paradox of the stone, divine omnipotence, Aquinas: philosophy of religion, Descartes: philosophy of religion, nonclassical logic

ISBNs: 9781009272407 (PB), 9781009272391 (OC)
ISSNs: 2754-8724 (online), 2754-8716 (print)

Contents

1 God's Stone Problem

Basic Beliefs: Logic and Theology

Most of us have some beliefs that are *basic* for us and some that are not. Basicality of belief is a matter of degree, determined across several different dimensions of evaluation. There are at least three marks by which we can determine whether and to what degree any given belief is basic for us (cf. Plantinga 1979/1983/2003). First, a belief's basicality is determined by conviction. The more firmly it is held, the more basic; the less firmly, the less basic. Second, a belief's basicality is determined by the extent to which it is supported by other beliefs. The fewer beliefs on the basis of which it is held, the more basic; the more, the less basic. And, third, a belief's basicality is determined by the extent to which it supports others; the more beliefs that are held on the basis of it, the more basic it is; the fewer, the less. The first of the three marks may be described as the belief's *credence*, whereas the second and third may be described as its *depth of ingression*. So understood, our most basic beliefs are those to which we give the greatest credence and that have the greatest depth of ingression in our belief-set. They are those in which we have staked the greatest doxastic investment.

Belief in the first principles of *logic* certainly meet these criteria of basicality. For example, we usually take as basic:

- the law of noncontradiction (LNC) $((p \wedge {\sim}p) \vdash \perp)$,
- the law of excluded middle (LEM) $({\sim}(p \vee {\sim}p) \vdash \perp)$,

and others (cf. Bittle 1953: ch. 2). Other rules of logical inference typically held as basic include:

- *reductio ad absurdum* (RAA) $((p \supset \perp) \vdash {\sim}p)$,
- *ex contradictione quodlibet* (ECQ, or *explosion*) $((p \wedge {\sim}p) \vdash q)$,
- disjunction elimination ($\vee$E) $((p \vee q), (p \supset r), (q \supset r) \vdash r)$,
- conjunction introduction ($\wedge$I) $(p, q \vdash (p \wedge q))$,
- *modus ponendo ponens* (MP) $((p \supset q), p \vdash q)$,
- *modus ponendo tollens* (MT) $((p \supset q), {\sim}q \vdash {\sim}p)$,
- existential introduction ($\exists$Ix) $(Fa \vdash \exists x(Fx))$,
- various categorical syllogisms (e.g., EAE-1) $({\sim}\exists x(Mx \wedge Px), \forall x(Sx \supset Mx) \vdash {\sim}\exists x(Sx \wedge Px))$,

and so on; and certain rules of logical semantics (i.e., immediate inference), such as the truth-value equivalence of eliminating, adding, or shifting around negation within quantifiers:

- $\forall x(p) \dashv\vdash \sim\exists x\sim(p),$
- $\exists x(p) \dashv\vdash \sim\forall x\sim(p)$

(cf. Bittle 1937; Lemmon 1965/1969; Kelley 1998; Barwise & Etchemendy 2002; Goldfarb 2003; Sider 2010; Bergmann, Moor, & Nelson 2014).

If the entire structure of our belief-set may be compared to a great spiderweb, our beliefs in the laws of logic, most analytic philosophers would say, sit snugly in the center (cf. Quine & Ullian 1970). These beliefs undoubtedly have some company, too. Certain of our mundane beliefs occupy a position very near the center, such as my belief that I am now typing on a keyboard. Were someone to ask me to demonstrate this, I would find myself struggling to find any other beliefs on the basis of which I hold it, in just the same way in which I would struggle to find a proof for the LNC. Certain of our ethical beliefs also sit very near to the center of our *noetic structures*. Were someone to ask me to prove, for example, that good is to be pursued and evil is to be avoided, or that there are indeed some cases of evil in the world, I would not know what to say to them. This goes similarly for certain of our metaphysical beliefs. For example, why do I believe in the law of sufficient causation (LSC) (necessarily, everything that exists has a cause for its existence)? I could probably come up with *some* answer. But any putative proof in my mouth would be no genuine reason for belief, since even if my proof were to fail, I would likely go on believing in it anyway. It is basic.

Most interestingly for present purposes, many analytic theologians likewise take the belief in *God* and the belief in certain other theological creeds to be properly basic, too. (Plantinga, famously, says that this holds true of him, as do other reformed epistemologists, mystical intuitionists, fideists, and "grammatical Thomists.") In fact, for some analytic theologians, beliefs about God and logic likely form the very core of their webs of belief, those in which they have the greatest doxastic investment, those beliefs which they take to be the *most basic* of all. Wittgenstein (1938/1966) noted as much. He writes that the devout theist seems almost to live in their own world, or play their own "language game," separate from the atheist or agnostic. The devout theist "has what you might call an unshakable belief. . . . This in one sense must be called the firmest of all beliefs because the man risks things on account of it, which he would not do on things which are far better established for him" (54). Moreover, the devout theist's belief "does not rest on the fact on which ordinary everyday beliefs do rest," but rests rather on "the belief as formulated on the evidence can only be the last result – in which a number of ways of thinking and acting [have already] crystalize[d] and come together" (56). Nonetheless, the devout theist constantly keeps this kind of theological "picture" before their mind, which influences all else that they believe and do. We'll return to this point momentarily.

Rational Paradox Resolution

Let's turn to the epistemic significance of basic beliefs, particularly as they relate to the rationality of *paradox resolution*. The term "paradox" has no neat definition. Sorensen (2004: 3–10) notes that a variety of different phenomena can rightly be called "paradoxes": riddles, visual illusions, aphorisms, conundrums, bodies of conflicting scientific evidence, antinomies, individual arguments, just the conclusion of certain arguments, just the premises of certain arguments, and so on. For present purposes, we'll focus exclusively on argumentative paradoxes, and so we'll define a *paradox* as any set of premises within an argument, each of which is thought to be independently plausible to some rational believer but apparently, collectively leads to an unacceptable contradiction (cf. Oms forthcoming). As this stipulative definition makes plain, a paradox is always a paradox relative to some believer, since what one person greets as a paradox, another may issue as a reductio (Lewis 1986/2005: 207).

When faced with a paradox, an epistemically conscientious person must attempt a resolution. This is because it is a minimal constraint on rationality that one makes one's belief-set as consistent as one can, and a paradox purports to show precisely that one's belief-set is presently inconsistent. Some paradoxes are better than others. The better are accompanied by arguments comprised of all and only deductively valid or inductively strong inferences. This forces the believer to deny at least one of the argument's premises, rather than merely rejecting the argument as a sophism or a mere *falsidicus* (cf. Quine 1961/1966). The better paradoxes also cite only premises which the intended target finds roughly equally plausible. In this way, the rational believer is forced to deny at least one of the argument's premises, but which they ought to deny is in no way obvious.

Again, if a person's belief-set may be compared to an intricate web, then a good paradox may be said to represent a big knot somewhere within its structure. The believer must cut some thread or other to resolve the tension. How should one proceed when attempting to resolve a good paradox? Plantinga's concept of basic belief may be of some service here. In general, when faced with a paradox, a rational agent should reject whichever of the argument's premises are *least basic* for them within their total belief-set. Carrying out this precept requires that the rational agent, first, determine their approximate credence in each of the paradox's premises, just considered on their own. Revising a belief in which one has high credence comes with a greater doxastic cost than revising one in which one has a lower credence. Second, the rational agent must consider those beliefs inward from each of the beliefs they are considering revising – that is, those beliefs on the basis of which they hold each of them individually. If a belief is logically entailed by any others, then revising it will mean also making additional changes elsewhere, which comes with greater doxastic cost. And, finally, the agent facing the paradox must also consider those beliefs outward from each of the beliefs they are considering revising – that is, those beliefs they hold on the basis of each of them individually. If a belief logically entails any others, then revising it will again mean making additional changes elsewhere. In this way, to follow a precept of revising one's least basic beliefs in the face of a good paradox is to follow a *maxim of minimum mutilation* (Quine 1986: 7, 85). To extend our economic metaphor, it is to take the most doxastically frugal option.

But the best paradoxes of all not only unfold validly and are comprised of premises that the intended audience finds equally plausible, but, what's more, they cite only premises that are among those most basic to the believer. Every paradox purports to demonstrate that a doxastic agent has a knot in their web, but the very best purport to show that the knot is right in the web's center. Even when perfectly following our maxim of minimum mutilation, a person in this position is in a sorry state, since it means that even the least drastic cut they can make is going to cut deep. A paradox that cites only a person's nonbasic beliefs is a puzzle to solve in one's spare time; a paradox that cites only a person's basic beliefs, on the other hand, is a "crisis in thought" (Quine 1961/1966: 7). Let's next turn to a few such excellent paradoxes for the analytic theist. Then I'll state this Element's purpose more explicitly.

Theological Paradoxes

There are many ways to classify paradoxes. Some are categorized according to their general argumentative structure, such as sorites paradoxes, which all, in one way or another, involve premises with vague predicates and operate according to a principle of inferential transitivity (cf. Bassford 2019). Others are categorized according to origination, such as the Eleatic paradoxes of Zeno of Elea (cf. Huggett 2019). And still others are categorized according to a principle of subject-domain specificity. In this way, we can speak of paradoxes of physics, metaphysical paradoxes, paradoxes of semantics, and – of especial interest here – *theological paradoxes*. All theological paradoxes are characterized by including at least one theological premise, such as the claim that God is omnibenevolent, that God created the world ex nihilo, or similar.

Theology is far from a homogenous discipline. Some infamous theological paradoxes are therefore not paradoxes for certain theologians at all. But the paradoxes I would like to detail here are all paradoxes for the tradition in which I will be operating: the tradition of *classical theism*. According to classical theism, there is one and only one god – namely, God. This is understood to be the same god of the revealed Abrahamic religions of Judaism, Christianity, and Islam. God is understood to have several highly distinctive *divine attributes*. All of the paradoxes that I will momentarily detail target these attributes. In summary, God is said to be a personal agent who is perfectly spiritual, perfectly free, perfectly simple, perfectly essential; omniscient, omnibenevolent, omnipresent, omnitemporal; impeccable, impassable, incomprehensible, infallible; whose existence is necessary; who exists *a se*; and who is the creator, sustainer, and governor of everything that exists so long as it exists (*extra Deum*) (cf. Anselm 1076/1975, 1077/1975; Al-Ghazali c. 1105/2016; Maimonides 1190/1956; Aquinas 1265, 1274/1952; Suárez 1597/1983; Descartes 1647/1996; Malebranche 1688/1997; Kenny 1979). And, most importantly here, God is also said to be essentially *omnipotent*.

There are many known theological paradoxes. They fall more or less neatly into two basic genera, each with two species of its own (to borrow – and expand upon – a taxonomy from Nagasawa 2008: 579–583). Most generally (Figure 1), some theological paradoxes are *pure* and some are *impure*. A pure theological paradox cites as premises only assumptions from theology and logic. An impure theological paradox cites as premises assumptions from theology and logic, but also at least one additional assumption from neither, such as an assumption from physics, metaphysics, or ethics.

There are two species of pure theological paradox: type-A and type-B. Type-A paradoxes target just one divine attribute. The most well-known type-A paradox is the *paradox of the stone*. (More on this one momentarily.) An additional type-A paradox is *Grim's paradox* (Grim 1983, 1984, 1990, 2000;

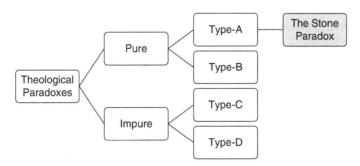

Figure 1 Varieties of theological paradox

Plantinga & Grim 1993) (not to be confused with the Grim Reaper paradox – cf. Koons 2014). Grim's paradox purports to show that belief in God is inconsistent with set theory, our logic of sets (cf. Fujii 1961/1963: chs. 6–10; Devlin 1992). It runs as follows. Classical theists say that God is essentially omniscient. So, he must know every true proposition, that is, the set of all truths. But, according to an easy application of Cantor's theorem, there could be no set of all truths. Consider the propositions that would be in this set: $\{p_1, p_2, p_3, \ldots \}$. A set is defined by its members, so let "T" be this set. For any set, we can always form its powerset. A powerset is defined as the set comprised of all the subsets generable from the elements of the initial set. So, the powerset of T, "P(T)," is the set defined as $\{\emptyset, \{p_1\}, \{p_2\}, \{p_3\}, \{p_1, p_2\}, \{p_1, p_3\}, \{p_2, p_3\}, \{p_1, p_2, p_3\}, \ldots \}$. Cantor proved that a powerset of a set always contains more members than the initial set. Now consider that there exists a unique truth corresponding to each element p of T – namely, whether or not $p \in T$. But this means that there are at least as many elements of T as there are of P(T), contradicting Cantor's theorem. Hence, there could be no omniscient being.

Type-B paradoxes are pure theological paradoxes that target more than one divine attribute. There are more known type-B paradoxes than type-A. They do not always have designated names, so we can name each according to the specific divine attributes involved in its premises. The *omnipotence-impeccability paradox* runs as follows. God is omnipotent, and so he can do anything. But God is impeccable, and so he cannot possibly fail at whatever he undertakes. Therefore, it would follow that God both can and cannot fail, which is absurd (cf. Conee 1991: 470, n. 3). The *omnipotence-omnibenevolence paradox*, again, points out that God can do anything. But, as omnibenevolent, God cannot possibly sin. Therefore, it would follow that God both can and cannot sin, which is absurd (cf. Pike 1969; Morriston 2001). The *omnipotence-impassability paradox*, again, reasons that God can do anything. But God is impassable, and so he cannot suffer. Therefore, it would follow that God both can and cannot suffer, which is absurd (cf. Hallman 1999). The *omniscience-impassibility* paradox starts from the premise that God knows everything. But as impassable, God cannot possibly know what it is to suffer firsthand. Therefore, God both knows and does not know what it is to suffer firsthand, which is absurd (cf. Blumenfeld 1978). Finally, the *omniscience-incomprehensibility paradox*, again, points out that God knows everything. But God is incomprehensible, and so his own nature cannot be fully known. Therefore, God both fully knows and does not fully know his own nature, which is absurd (cf. Creel 1980). And further type-B paradoxes can be generated, as well. The divine attribute of *omnipotence* would seem to be especially pernicious for generating type-B paradoxes, since if indeed God can do anything, then one might think he can do or be precisely the opposite of what he can do and essentially is (cf. Hill 2014).

There are likewise two species of impure theological paradox: type-C and type-D. Type-C paradoxes cite at least one theological premise, some assumptions about logic, and, finally, some nontheological, nonlogical premise about a *contingent* fact of reality. Theologians have traditionally been the most exercised by type-C paradoxes. Two are notorious. The first is the *paradox of evil*. The characteristic nontheological, nonlogical premise of the paradox of evil is the claim that evil (or suffering) exists in the world, which it is said is incompatible with the divine nature. Epicurus (c. 300 BC) offers the classic representation of the problem, cast as a series of rhetorical questions: "Is God willing to prevent evil but not able? Then he is impotent. Is he able but not willing? Then he is malevolent. Is he both willing and able? Then whence comes evil? Is he neither willing nor able? Then why call him 'God'?" (in Pojman 2003: 137; cf. also Lactanitius c. 300/1871: chs. 4, 8–10, 13, 15, 17). Hill (1998: 32) reports that over 3,600 articles and books have been written on the paradox of evil between 1960 and c. 2000 alone, and the number has continued to grow. A few responses to this problem are worth noting for later. Augustine of Hippo (c. 397/1961: ch. 7) thinks the argument is valid, and so he denies one of its premises: that evil actually exists in the world. His reasoning is that evil is merely privation, whereas only goodness has positive reality. Consequently, it is strictly speaking improper to say that evil exists, since all evil is merely the absence of goodness (cf. Bittle 1939: ch. 14). More commonly, others deny that the paradox is valid and contend that the existence of evil in the world is compatible with God's nature just in case there's a good reason why he permits evil to exist (cf. Antony 2018). Al-Ghazali (c. 1105/ 2016, ch. 3) and Hick (1963: 40–46), for example, hold that our world is a kind of *testing ground*, where God observes and evaluates our behavior for the sake of determining who is deserving of Heaven and who is deserving of Hell. Plantinga (1967: chs. 5–6, 1977), on the other hand, holds that the reason God allows evil in the world is because of the superseding value of free will, which makes the existence of evil worth it. This is usually coupled with a defense according to which it is not God who is responsible for the world's evils, but rather us and the wicked use of our free will (cf. Lewis 1940/1962; Stump 1985). In this way, God is blameless for existent evil; he could nonetheless stop it or otherwise prevent it if he so willed it, but the existence of free will is such a great good that, in his omniscience, he has determined that the evil is necessary.

However, the second most notorious type-C paradox is the *paradox of foreknowledge*. The characteristic nontheological, nonlogical premise of the paradox of foreknowledge is the claim that we have free will, which, it is said, is incompatible with God's nature. An informal demonstration of this runs as follows. God is omniscient, so he knows everything, including what will happen at every time in the future. God is infallible, and so he cannot possibly be mistaken about what will happen in the future. So, what will happen in the future must necessarily happen. But we have free will, and so what we will choose to do in the future is not necessary, since otherwise we would not be free to either do or not do anything (cf. Frankfurt 1969). From this, it follows that God must both know and not know what we will freely choose to do in the future, which is absurd (cf. Boethius 524/1999: bk. 5, chs. 3–4; Hunt & Zagzebski 2022). There are many known theistic replies to this paradox, but I'll recount just one which will be relevant later. Molina (1588/1988: disp. 22, sect. 9) argues that there are several distinct types of divine knowledge, and the type of knowledge by which God knows what we will freely do in the future is compatible with free will. God has *middle knowledge* (*scientia media*) of what we will freely choose to do. Divine middle knowledge means only that God knows what we *would* do, *were* some antecedent state to occur, for any given antecedent state (cf. Flint 1983, 1998; Hasker 1989: ch. 2). As Saadia Gaon (933/1984) explains:

> Should it be asked, therefore: "But if God foreknows that a human being will speak, is it conceivable that he should remain silent?" We would answer simply that . . . [i]t would not be proper to assume that God knows that that person will speak, because what God foreknows is the final *denouement* of man's activity as it turns out after all his planning, anticipations, and delays. It is that very thing that God knows. (bk. 4, ch. 6)

Finally, type-D paradoxes are theological paradoxes that cite at least one theological premise, some assumptions about logic, and, finally, at least one premise hailing from neither theology nor logic making some claim about a *necessary* fact of reality, such as a law of nature or an established metaphysical theory (perhaps also in conjunction with a premise about a contingent fact of reality). Historically, the most popular type-D paradox has been the *paradox of creatio* ex nihilo. It runs as follows. God is said to be the creator of everything that exists (*extra Deum*). Moreover, God's creation is said to be distinct from creaturely creation, which is really only a type of modification; God is supposed to have created everything *from nothing* (cf. Bonaventure 1259/1978: sect. 14; Bittle 1953: 300–316; Devenish 1985). But metaphysicians since Parmenides (c. 475 BC) have traditionally held that *ex nihilo nihil fit* (ENN) (necessarily, nothing comes from nothing). Consequently, it would follow that God both created everything from nothing and that he could not have created anything from nothing, which is absurd (cf. Burrus 2013).

More recently, metaphysically inclined analytic theologians have been exercised by the *paradox of necessary existence*. It runs as follows. God is said to be a necessary being (cf. Pruss & Rasmussen 2018). Moreover, God is said, again, to be the creator of everything (*extra Deum*). Now, according to *modal realism*, our reality is only one segment of a whole comprised of many other possible realities (*possible worlds*), all equally real. All possible worlds are causally isolated from one another, and to say that something "possibly exists" is to say that there is a possible world at which that thing exists (cf. Lewis 1986). So, to say that God is a "necessary being" means that he must exist at *every* possible world. But creation is a causal relation. Consequently, if God, the creator, exists at every possible world, then every possible world is causally related after all. So, God both necessarily exists and also does not necessarily exist, which is absurd (cf. Collier 2019; Bassford 2021a). And other type-D paradoxes can be generated as well.

The Stone Paradox (Informal Presentation)

Let's take stock. We began with a discussion of basic beliefs and observed that the typical analytic theist takes as basic their beliefs in logic, theology, and a host of others pertaining to metaphysics, epistemology, axiology, and so on. We then discussed the notion of a paradox and stated criteria according to which a paradox is most *dialectically felicitous* – viz., whenever it is valid, cites premises equally plausible to its intended target, and moreover cites as premises only basic beliefs of the target. We said that a rational method for resolving such paradoxes is to follow the maxim of minimum mutilation, according to which we ought to greet such paradoxes by striving to jettison whichever belief expressed in the paradox's premises is least basic for us. Finally, we considered a few such excellent paradoxes for the analytic theist and stated how they all logically hang together in terms of being pure or impure, being type-A, type-B, type-C, or type-D.

I can now state what is the proper subject of this Element, why it is so theologically significant and logically fascinating, and how the rest of the Element will accordingly proceed. The subject of this Element is the *paradox of the stone*. This is a pure paradox of theology, in that it cites as premises only assumptions from classical theology and classical logic. Moreover, it is a type-A paradox, in that it targets only one divine attribute – the most troublemaking of the bunch – *divine omnipotence*.

I'll start with two prosaic presentations of the paradox, one from Mavrodes, and one from Frankfurt, since Mavrodes and Frankfurt were two of the earliest respondents to the stone paradox in contemporary philosophy of religion, and their responses are representative of the two major ways careful analytic theists have since approached the problem. (More on this momentarily.) Mavrodes (1963: 221):

> [C]an God create a stone too heavy for Him to lift? This appears to ... pose a dilemma. If we say that God can create a stone, then it seems that there might be such a stone. And if there might be a stone too heavy for Him to lift, then He is evidently not omnipotent. But if we deny that God can create such a stone, we seem to have given up His omnipotence already. Both answers lead to the same conclusion.

Frankfurt (1964: 262):

> The puzzle suggests a test of God's power – can He create a stone too heavy for Him to lift? – which, it seems, cannot fail to reveal that His power is limited. For He must, it would appear, either show His limitations by being unable to create such a stone or by being unable to lift it once He had created it.

Now I'll offer a semiformal demonstration of the paradox (cf., e.g., Englebretsen 1971). The paradox of the stone runs:

1. God is omnipotent.
2. Either God can create a stone too heavy for him to lift, or he cannot.
3. If God can create the unliftable stone, then he is not omnipotent, since unable to lift the stone. [First Horn]
4. If God cannot create the unliftable stone, then he is not omnipotent, since unable to create the stone. [Second Horn]
5. Therefore, God is not omnipotent. [From (2), (3), & (4)]
6. But this is absurd. [From (1) & (5); QED]

Premise (1) is just a statement of divine omnipotence. Premise (2) is just an application of LEM. Premises (3) and (4) are thought to be derivable from (1) and (2) with minimal, valid applications of deductive inference rules. Line (5) would follow then from an instance of ∨E. And (6) would follow from an application of ∧I, which then violates the LNC. But RAA tells us that if a set of assumptions leads to a contradiction, then we must deny one of our initial assumptions. Our only initial assumptions here are divine omnipotence, LEM, and a few other inference rules. And so, this paradox would purport to show that one must modify either their theology or their logic.

   To my mind, the stone paradox is the purest, most difficult theological paradox, even among other type-A paradoxes. That God's omniscience requires his knowing the *set of all truths* is not basic within my noetic structure; and so Quine's maxim of minimum mutilation would advise that I resolve Grim's paradox by rejecting that premise. The LEM, the LNC, and the rest of the logical apparatus involved in the stone paradox, on the other hand, certainly are most basic within my belief-set. Moreover, the thorniest of the type-B paradoxes appear to be those involving omnipotence, such as the omnipotence-omnibenevolent paradox. This suggests that, if we can resolve the stone paradox, which is often just simply called the *omnipotence paradox* (cf. Cowan 1965, 1974; Rosenkrantz & Hoffman 2022), then those other paradoxes may find eventual resolution, too. But how best to resolve the stone paradox is in no way obvious. It is an excellent paradox, and the epistemically conscientious analytic theist should be vexed. More than the rest, this is a paradox of *theo* and *logica*, God and logic. In the face of it, ought the theist to diagnose the dilemma as a *problem of God* or a *problem of logic*? Ought they to lose their religion or lose their mind?

I set out in this Element to complete two tasks. The first is pedagogical. The stone paradox and its near variants have been around for nearly two millennia, with the earliest formulations (probably) occurring in the writings of the early medievals, such as Origen of Alexandria (c. 230/1966) and Pseudo-Dionysius the Areopagite (c. 500/1897). Omnipotence paradoxes reached a high point in the late medieval period and exercised the best logically minded classical theologians of the middle ages, such as Anselm of Canterbury (1077/ 1975), Maimonides (1190/1956), Aquinas (1274/1952), Scotus (c. 1300/1987), William of Ockham (1318/1979), et al. Divine omnipotence received some additional analyses in the early modern period, puzzling classical theistic philosophers like Descartes (1641/2006, 1647/1996, 1629–1649/1970) and Malebranche (1688/1997). Work on the stone paradox then lay dormant for some years, finding occasional reference only in the scholastic and neo-scholastic Catholic manuals (but see McTaggart 1906: ch. 6, sect. 166), until Mackie (1955) forcefully reintroduced the problem into contemporary analytic theology. Since then, conversation surrounding omnipotence paradoxes has again continued uninterrupted and has now reached another great state of philosophical maturity. However, while there are some surveys of the contemporary responses to the paradox available, there exists no fully comprehensive examination of past responses, nor does there exist a formal demonstration that the paradox is valid. And so, I set out in this Element, first, to fill that deficit.

The second task of this Element is dialectical. I will attempt to resolve the paradox in accordance with the maxim of minimum mutilation. I believe the paradox is valid, as I'll demonstrate momentarily. So, the analytic theist is indeed forced to choose whether to revise a principle of theology or a principle of logic. Those following the lead of Aquinas (e.g., Mavrodes 1963) opt to revise their theology in the face of the paradox. Those following Descartes (e.g.,

Frankfurt 1964) opt to revise their logic in the face of it. Both hope to make minimal revisions such that the analytic theist can continue to maintain their faith in both. I'll adopt the Cartesian stance and argue that the analytic theist should expand their conception of modal space: God can violate the laws of logic and thereby do the absolutely impossible, if he wills. The descriptive name of this position is *weak dialetheic classical theism*, and I'll motivate it by considering how it can circumvent famous objections to the Thomistic resolution of the paradox, while at the same time avoiding the problems of its near cousin, strong dialectic classical theism. Applied to the stone paradox, this means that I will be targeting premise (3) discussed earlier in this section. In effect, I claim that God could create a stone so heavy that even he can't lift it . . . but he might nonetheless lift it anyway! In Section 2, I'll explore and criticize the Thomistic reply; in Section 3, I'll explore and defend the Cartesian one. (N.B. "Thomism" and "Cartesianism" denote other positions in other debates. For the sake of this Element, I assume no affinity between these positions.)

"Can Do" Logic

A few precisifying remarks are in order before beginning. The semiformal presentation of the stone paradox given earlier is potentially problematic in several respects. Some objections to it, as it stands, are sound, and they point the way to a better version of the paradox. Other objections are not, but they too point the way to stating the problem in its strongest form. Additionally, I have said that there are really only two ways of rationally resolving the paradox: the Thomistic line and the Cartesian line. I should justify that claim, too, since it is not immediately obvious why this is so.

First, one might object to the paradox on the grounds that its second premise is not actually a valid instance of LEM. It is mere *nonsense*. What do we mean in saying that "God can do anything"? Given that we are speaking of what God "can do," one might think that we should understand this claim to mean that God can successfully undertake any *action*. This means we must understand God's omnipotence according to a *logic of action*. But, according to Swinburne (1973: 231) and Morris (1991: 66–67), among others, there is no such thing as an impossible action. To be an action means to be possibly performable, and so anything that is necessarily unperformable simply fails to be an action at all and is rather a mere "pseudo-task" (Miller in Londey, Miller, & King-Farlow 1971: 30). But no paradox follows from any ill-formed formula. Therefore, the stone paradox is in need of not resolution but rather *dissolution*.

This is not a sound response to the paradox. Two things should be said in reply to it. First, we should not follow a logic of action that does not permit impossibilities as values of action-variables. Consider some claim about an agent performing a putatively impossible task: "Thomas Hobbes successfully squared a circle." This proposition is false, because its negation is true, namely that "Hobbes did not successfully square a circle." But the negation of nonsense is not truth, but rather just more nonsense. And, second, an action-logic is neither necessary nor preferable for expressing the stone paradox anyway. A better logic for the job is a mixed predicate Kripkean modal logic, permitting quantification over propositions and inter-categorical relations between objects and propositions, and with a built-in "actualization" dyadic predicate. A logic like this allows us to better express divine omnipotence and also grants us the ability to deduce the paradox's contradiction in a more intuitively satisfying way, given how it is usually expressed by the atheologian.

I will assume the reader is familiar with propositional logic and quantified predicate logic. *Quantified propositional logic*, then, allows us to quantify over propositions, too – for example, "$\exists\varphi(\varphi)$," read as: "There is some proposition, φ, such that φ obtains"; and "$\forall\varphi(\varphi)$," read as: "For all propositions, φ, φ obtains" (cf. Uzquiano 2020: sect. 3.5; Thomason 1980; Fine 1970). *Mixed predicate logic* allows us to express as well-formed formulae propositions in the language of both propositional and predicate logic. So, in this logic, propositions of the form "F(a)" are well formed, as are simpler propositions of the form "p." (A single sentence letter on its own, then, should be understood to mean that a certain proposition – named "p" – obtains.) Combining the two logics, we can allow ourselves the following inference rule:

- propositional existential introduction ($\exists I\varphi$) (p ⊢ $\exists\varphi(\varphi)$),

since if it is the case that "p" is the case, then it is also the case that something is the case. Our quantified propositional logic should also afford us the following rules:

- propositional existential elimination ($\exists E\varphi$) ($\exists\varphi(\varphi)$ ⊢ p),

when "p" is a new, arbitrary, atomic proposition within the domain; and:

- propositional universal elimination ($\forall E\varphi$) ($\forall\varphi(\varphi)$ ⊢ p),

when "p" is either a novel atomic proposition or one already recognized within the domain. (For technical issues having to do with the logic's consistency, the elimination rules should be restricted to only truth-functionally simple propositions, and our quantifier introduction rules ought only to quantify over propositions whose primary operator is not already a propositionally quantified proposition – cf. Russell 1903/1965: appx. B, sect. 500; Linsky 1999: ch. 4, sect. 2.)

Modal logic allows us to symbolize and reason with modal propositions, that is, propositions expressing what could be the case, what must be the case, what could not be the case, and so on (cf. Beall & van Fraassen 2003). Modal logic treats these intensive parts of ordinary speech as propositional operators, such that we can write "◇p" to express that p is possibly the case, "□p" to express that p must be the case, and "~◇p" to express that it is impossible that p is the case. *Kripkean modal logic*, then, gives us a set of inference rules and a *possible worlds* semantics for modal propositions (cf. Kripke 1959, 1963a, 1963b). (I have already mentioned possible worlds in the context of modal realism and the paradox of necessary existence. One needn't accept modal realism, which is a metaphysical theory of possible worlds, in order to accept Kripkean semantics for modal logic.) A possible world, for present purposes, can be understood as a maximal set of propositions – a set of propositions such that, for every proposition that there is, either it or its negation is in the set. It is a complete picture of the way things could be. There are many such sets, and whereas a proposition may be true in one world, it needn't be true in another. Consequently, modal logic is a logic of shifting universal domains (cf. Yagisawa 1992), moving the reasoner from world to world.

Kripkean modal semantics changes our logic's syntax; every proposition must accordingly be indexed to some particular world. So, in this logic, "p" is ill formed, but rather we must say, "<p, w>," where "w" is the particular possible world at which $v(p) = 1$. What does it mean to say that "<◇p, w>"? To account for true modal propositions, Kripke introduces the concept of an *accessibility relation* between worlds. To say that some proposition is possibly true at w is to say that there exists some other world, "w*," such that w* is "accessible" from (bears a certain kind of relation to) w, and $v(<p, w*>) = 1$. Put more concisely, we get the inference rule:

- Kripkean semantics (K) <◇p, w> ⊣⊢ ∃w*(R(w, w*) ∧ (<p, w*>))

In this way, Kripkean modal semantics has allowed us to partially reduce modal propositions to equivalent extensional ones (cf. Quine 1947). Moreover, it has allowed us to correct the modal logic of Aristotle (c. 350 BCa: *Prior Analytics*, bk. 1, chs. 8–15; Burdian c. 1335/1985: bk. 2), as well as verify and radically expand our stock of known valid modal inference rules (cf. Lewis & Langford 1932; Priest 2008a). We need to mention only three for the sake of formalizing the stone paradox later:

- modal reflexivity (MR) (<□p, w> ⊢ R(w, w), <p, w>),
- necessity elimination (□E) (<□p, w>, R(w, w*) ⊢ <p, w*>),
- possibility elimination (◇E) (<◇p, w> ⊢ ∃w*(R(w, w*)), <p, w*>),

where w* is not already in our domain of discourse and so is a novel witness to the affirmed possibility. This is the modal logic "T," which is uncontroversial (cf. Sider 2010: ch. 6). We'll therefore allow certain other semantic equivalences obtaining between necessity and possibility claims, which we'll simply call our "Equiv." rules in the following proof:

- $\Box p \dashv\vdash \sim\Diamond\sim p$,
- $\Diamond p \dashv\vdash \sim\Box\sim p$

Finally, the best logic for representing the stone paradox must also include *inter-categorical relations* obtaining between objects and propositions within the domain – in particular, a relation of *actualization*. This is our way of saying that an object "can do" something, without needing an action-logic. Instead of speaking of "tasks" or "actions," we can instead understand the claim that some agent can do something as the claim that the agent can actualize a state of affairs; or, put with less ontological commitment, that an agent can make true some proposition (cf. Schrader 1979). Where "α" is an agent and "p" is some state that we wish to say α *brings about*, we write "$<A(\alpha, p), w>$," read as: "At world w, α makes it the case that p obtains." Bringing in our modal operators, we can then write that α *can* bring about p as: $<\Diamond A(\alpha, p), w>$. This inter-categorical relation comes with an important inference rule:

- actualization elimination (AE) ($<A(\alpha, p), w> \vdash <p, w>$)

The rationale for this rule is that "actualization" is a factive relation, and so if an agent actualizes a proposition, then that proposition must obtain; otherwise they have not really actualized it.

We should revisit our ∃Iφ rule in light of our addition of modal logic and inter-categorical relations. It would seem that ∃Iφ can be applied to any proposition in which a proposition is a constituent component, including instances in which the proposition is embedded within our actualization relation. So, the following inference is a valid instance of AE:

$$<A(\alpha, p), w> \vdash <\exists\varphi(A(\alpha, \varphi)), w>$$

It would seem not to make any difference if the proposition is flagged with an object-quantifier. So, this is valid:

$$<\exists x(A(x, p), w> \vdash <\exists\varphi\exists x(A(x, \varphi)), w>$$

Nor does it make any difference whether the actualization relation is stated to be the case or is only possibly the case. And so, per ∃Iφ, inferences of this form are valid, too:

$$<\Diamond A(\alpha, p), w> \vdash <\exists\varphi\Diamond A(\alpha, \varphi), w>$$

Finally, the proposition our existential quantifier is capturing within the inter-categorical relation can be of any level of complexity, and in either propositional or predicate syntax.

As the reader can see, this is a very expressively powerful logic. But it is no more expressively powerful than necessary, and it allows us to state precisely what we mean to say in saying that "God can do anything." Letting "Θ" stand for God, and letting "w" stand for the actual world, this is the claim that:

$$<\forall\varphi\Diamond A(\Theta, \varphi), w>,$$

read as: "For all propositions, φ, it is possible for God to make φ the case." (This translation assumes that "can do" implies "possibly does." This may be a controversial assumption, but a defense now would take the Element too far off course – cf. Talbott 1988; Pearce 2021.) Additionally, this logic allows us to express well the stone paradox's dilemma. Letting "p" stand for the proposition "There is a stone too heavy for God to lift" (for simplification), the disjunction expressed in premise (2) is:

$$<(\Diamond A(\Theta, p)) \vee \sim(\Diamond A(\Theta, p)), w>$$

Failures of Sense and Reference

Alternatively, one might object to the paradox on linguistics ground. First, one might say that the paradox suffers from a failure of *reference*. The stone paradox does not just ask whether God can make any arbitrary proposition, p, true, but rather a very specific one: whether it is possible that "God creates a certain stone too heavy for him to lift." Let's call that stone "σ." But the problem is that "σ" does not actually refer to anything; a fortiori, it could not even possibly refer to anything, since given that God has unlimited lifting power, a stone too heavy for God to lift would need to possess infinite mass, which is impossible (cf. Wertz 1984). So, King-Farlow points out, any proposition in which "σ" is a constituent term suffers from *referential failure* and is therefore false, as Aristotle teaches us (in Londey, Miller, & King-Farlow 1971: 31–33; cf. Aristotle c. 350 BC/1941a: *Categories*, ch. 10, 13b 20–25). (But see *Categories*, ch. 10, 13b 26ff; also Russell 1905; Lewis 1978). Similarly, Devnish (1985: 112ff) complains that the paradox suffers from a failure of *sense*. The paradox asks whether God could "create" a stone too heavy for him to lift. But divine creation is entirely distinct from creaturely creation, and no one fully understands it. To pose a paradox couched in terms that neither oneself nor one's interlocutor really understands is dialectically fallacious and proves nothing.

In reply, I'll say that the scope of both solutions is too narrow to resolve the dilemma. The canonical version of the stone paradox speaks of stones and acts of creating and lifting. But the disjunctive premise of the paradox is merely one application of LEM. Other applications would serve equally well here. For example, instead of asking whether God could create an unliftable stone, we could just as well ask, with Mackie (1955: 210): "Can [God] make things which he cannot subsequently control? Or, what is practically equivalent to this, can [God] make rules which then bind himself?" Alternatively, we might ask: Could God square a circle? Could God finish traversing a staircase with infinite steps (cf. Juster 1961)? Could God correctly calculate that $2 + 2 = 5$? Could God pet a cat so aloof that even he can't pet it? Could God pose himself a paradox so difficult that even he can't resolve it? Or, in what is probably the paradox's purest form: Could God ever *deny himself*? (cf. 2 Timothy 2:13; Pseudo-Dionysus c. 500/1897: ch. 8, sect. 6). All of these versions of the paradox would seem to make the same point, so the best representation of the stone paradox should encapsulate them all in one shot. Accordingly, I propose that what the stone paradox is really asking is:

$$\diamond A(\Theta, (\sim\diamond A(\Theta, p)))?$$

where "p" is any proposition whatsoever. This is the question: Could God make it the case that he cannot make it the case that something is the case? Or, what is practically equivalent to this, can God make it the case that he is not omnipotent:

$$\diamond A(\Theta, (\sim\forall\varphi(\diamond A(\Theta, \varphi))))?$$

Contingent Omnipotence

Alternatively, one might object to the stone paradox on the grounds that it is invalid, as follows. Given our current statement of omnipotence, the first horn does not lead to a contradiction. A contradiction would follow only if the first premise stated that God is *necessarily* omnipotent. So, if God is merely *contingently* omnipotent, then the problem is resolved (cf., e.g., Sobel 2004: ch. 9). Suppose that, at our world, w, God is contingently omnipotent (i.e., omnipotent but not necessarily omnipotent). And now suppose also that he can create an unliftable stone. Given this second premise, it would follow in our modal logic that there is a world, w*, such that, at w*, God creates the unliftable stone. The stone is unliftable; consequently God cannot lift it at w*. But that is no problem. At w, God can do anything, whereas at w*, he cannot. Or, put modally, God is actually omnipotent, but he is possibly impotent. This is not a contradiction; this is just what it is to have a property contingently.

This is a sound objection to the stone paradox, as it stands. The stone paradox proponent must revise their first premise. Instead of (1), they should say: (1*) Necessarily, God is omnipotent (i.e., necessarily, he can do anything):

$$<\Box\forall\varphi\Diamond A(\Theta, \varphi), w>$$

Proposition (1*) entails (1), per MR; moreover, this premise is strong enough to close the logical gap in the original paradox, as will be demonstrated formally later. The critic has shown that the stone paradox is not genuinely a paradox of omnipotence per se, but a *paradox of necessary omnipotence*.

One might think that this goes to show that the analytic theist should not accept the proposition that God is necessarily omnipotent. But this tack is not available to the classical theologian. Classical theism contends that God is essentially omnipotent; a fortiori, it contends that God has every property he has essentially. But it is a necessary consequence of having a property essentially that one has it necessarily (cf. Plantinga 1970; Fine 1994; Bassford 2022a). The analytic theist might even treat the belief that God is necessarily omnipotent as basic. But if they do not, the stone paradox proponent could offer any number of arguments to demonstrate this. Here's one. Per *divine simplicity*, God is perfectly simple. Classical theologians take this to mean that God is not simply living, wise, good, or strong, as though these were various properties that God possesses, separate from himself. But rather, as St. Anselm (1077/1975) puts it: "But surely whatever You [i.e., God] are You are through no other than through Yourself. Therefore, You are the life by which You live, the wisdom by which You comprehend, and the goodness by which You are good both to those who are good and to those who are evil, and similarly for similar attributes" (*Proslogion*, ch. 12). So, God does not relate to his divine attributes in terms of predicate and subject, property and object, but rather in terms of *identity* between God and the divine attributes themselves (cf. Brower 2008; Adams 2015: 770). God is therefore identical to his omnipotence. But the law of identity (LOI) tells us that, necessarily, everything is identical to itself. Consequently, God is necessarily omnipotent, too. It is therefore a dialectically acceptable modification to the stone paradox to revise (1) for (1*).

McTaggartism and Cusanism

One final remark before getting underway. I have said there are only two ways one might attempt to rationally resolve the stone paradox. The *Thomistic solution*, following Aquinas (1274/1952, et al.), attempts to blunt the second

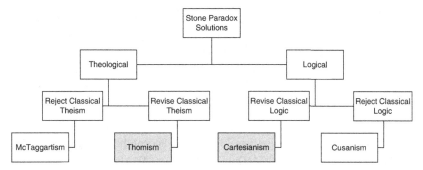

Figure 2 Stone paradox solutions

horn. The Thomists argue that God's inability to create an unliftable stone is no threat to classical theism. The *Cartesian solution*, on the other hand, following Descartes (1629–1649/1970), attempts to blunt the first horn. The Cartesians argue that God's ability to potentially lift an unliftable stone is no threat to classical logic. But one might object that there are not only two options for resolution here. At least two additional solutions have been inexplicably snubbed (Figure 2).

Geach (1973: 7ff) argues that the analytic theist should flatly reject premise (1), that God is omnipotent (cf. also Cowan 1965). (Consequently, they should also reject premise (1*), which is even stronger.) Assuming "omnipotence" can be defined at all (cf. La Croix 1977), Geach argues that the claim that God is "omnipotent" is merely a matter of "theological etiquette." When the Greek Church Fathers, et al., spoke of God's power, they did not use the term "omnipotent" but rather "παντοκράτωρ" (*pantokrator*), which, used as a title, translates best to "ruler of all," and when used as an adjective, "παντοκρατής" (*pantokrates*), is better translated to "almighty" or "supreme." (In Aeschylus 467 BC: "Seven Against Thebes," l. 255, for example, Zeus, king of the gods, is given this epithet: "ὦ παγκρακές Ζεῦ!") This phrase was Latinized as "*omnipotens*," which classically had the same connotation (Lewis 1940/1962: 26, n. 1). However, sometime between the late twelfth through early fourteenth centuries, the term "omnipotens" underwent significant semantic drift. Instead of connoting power "*over*" all things or power "*in*" all things, it came to mean power "*to do*" all things (cf. Leftow 2011, 2012). Our English word "omnipotence" has unfortunately inherited this semantic drift. So, the more classical commitment of classical theism is only the commitment that God is *almighty*, not that he is *omnipotent*. Moreover, if one scans the scriptures of the revealed Abrahamic religions, they are more likely to encounter claims about God's awesome might or strength, rather than his ability to do anything: for instance, "Your arm is endued with power; your hand is strong, your right hand exalted"

(Psalms 89:13); "Lord, . . . nothing is too hard for you" (Jeremiah 32:17); "[B]e strong in the Lord, and in the power of his might" (Ephesians 6:10); and so on. So, we can reject premise (1) without fear of losing sight of classical theism, since classical theology never really intended to contend that God "can do all things" anyway, but only, as is refrained throughout the Qur'an, that "God is *strong*" (8:52; 11:66; 22:40, and so on.). Since Geach reports that he was inspired by remarks from McTaggart (1906: chs. 6–7), we can call those who follow Geach et al. "McTaggartists," those who accept the *McTaggartist solution* to the stone paradox (cf. McDaniel 2020: sect. 4). McTaggart: "In calling [God] supreme, I do not mean to assert that he is omnipotent, but that he is, at the least, much more powerful than any other being, and so powerful that his volition can profoundly affect the whole sum of existence" (ch. 6, sect. 152).

A fourth strategy of response to the paradox is to reject either premise (2), and so with it the LEM, or otherwise to accept that some contradictions are true, and so reject the LNC. Either way, this means rejecting certain fundamental axioms and theorems from classical logic (including, importantly, ECQ) (cf. Beall & Ripley 2004). Beall and Cotnoir (2017) take the first tack and defend a position of *strong analetheic classical theism*. Analetheism states that there either are or might be genuine analetheia. An analetheia is a proposition that is *neither true nor false* (also called "gappy"), a proposition which therefore violates the LEM. Strong analetheists say that there are actual analetheia, whereas weak say there merely could be. Applied to classical theism, Beall and Cotnoir contend that some theological propositions are actual analetheia, and they think the stone paradox demonstrates that this is so: Witness premise (2). Cotnoir (2017) takes the second tack and defends a position of *strong dialetheic classical theism* (cf. also Ahsan 2022). Dialetheism states that there either are or might be genuine dialetheia. A dialetheia is a proposition that is *both true and false* (also called "glutty"), a proposition that therefore violates the LNC. Strong dialetheists say that there are actual dialetheia, whereas weak say there merely could be. Applied to classical theism, Cotnoir contends that some theological propositions are actual dialetheia, and he thinks the stone paradox demonstrates that this is so: Witness lines (1) and (5). Both analetheism and dialetheism are species of the broader category of *paraconsistentism* (i.e., any logic that denies ECQ) (cf. Priest, Tanaka, & Weber 2022). Cartesianism is a form of weak paraconsistentism. So, let's call those who accept a strongly paraconsistentist solution to the stone paradox "Cusanists," those who accept the *Cusanist solution* to the stone paradox, in honor of Nicholas of Cusa (1440/1969: esp. chs. 2–3), the most well-known historical supporter of strong paraconsistent classical theism (cf. Priest, Berto, & Weber 2018: sect. 2; Miller 2021). Nicholas: "[T]here is one sole Maximum [viz., God] which embraces all things – the maximum, which is also the minimum, and in which the inclusion of diversity in identity is not a contradiction."

So, the critic is right that two possible replies to the paradox have been excluded. But, to the McTaggartists, specifically: Geach's reply to the stone paradox is not in fact consistent with classical theism. Perhaps as a result of another instance of semantic drift, "classical theism" does currently entail a commitment to divine omnipotence. Aquinas (1274/1952) ensured this. So, to accept the McTaggartist reply is to deny classical theism, perhaps in favor of a nonclassical theism with even more ancient roots than it. Second, even if the early Abrahamic theists did not use the term "omnipotence," we can still find passages in scripture that claim that God can do all things. For example: "Lord, I know that You can do all things and that no plan of Yours can be thwarted" (Job 42:1–2); "Nothing is impossible for God" (Luke 1:37); "[W]ith God all things are possible" (Matthew 19:26); and so on.

And to both the McTaggartists and the Cusanists: To accept either of their solutions to the stone paradox over the Thomistic or Cartesian solutions is to run afoul of Quine's maxim of minimum mutilation. Both McTaggartism and Thomism are species of theological reply to the stone paradox. However, whereas the McTaggartist would force the analytic theist to reject classical theology, the Thomist suggests only that they *revise* their theology so as to at least preserve the letter of it. (N.B. The Thomist would not describe themself as revising the doctrine of divine omnipotence, but rather only *clarifying* it. But from the perspective of what "omnipotence" would seem on its face to mean, this nonetheless amounts to a revision.) Similarly, both Cusanism and Cartesianism are species of logical reply to the stone paradox. However, whereas the Cusanist would force the analytic theologian to reject classical logic, the Cartesian suggests only that they revise their logic so as to at least preserve the letter of it. (The Cusanist says that classical logic is not the law of our reality, whereas the Cartesian says it is.) The Thomistic and Cartesian solutions are therefore less doxastically costly and at least purport to allow the analytic theist to maintain their basic beliefs with minimal revisions. McTaggartism and Cusanism are therefore fallback positions, at best.

The Stone Paradox (Formal Presentation)

At this point, we have now stated everything to fully appreciate the difficulty of the paradox and to offer a precise demonstration of its formal validity. I'll use a modified modal semantic tableaux method (i.e., a truth tree) to demonstrate its validity, since this type of proof system essentially indexes propositions to worlds, which will be important in my reply to it later (cf. Bergmann, Moor, & Nelson 2014: chs. 4, 9; Beall & van Fraassen 2003: ch. 5; Priest 2008a: chs. 1–3, 12, 14–15).

Proof 1 Disjunctive form

i.	$\Box\forall\varphi\Diamond A(\Theta, \varphi), w$	A; Omnipotence
ii.	$\Diamond A(\Theta, (\sim\Diamond A(\Theta, p))) \vee \sim\Diamond A(\Theta, (\sim\Diamond A(\Theta, p))), w$	A; LEM
iii.	$\Diamond A(\Theta, (\sim\Diamond A(\Theta, p))), w$	A; per VE
iv.	$R(w, w^*)$	iii; $\Diamond$E
v.	$A(\Theta, (\sim\Diamond A(\Theta, p))), w^*$	iii; $\Diamond$E
vi.	$\sim\Diamond A(\Theta, p), w^*$	v; AE
vii.	$\exists\varphi\sim\Diamond A(\Theta, \varphi), w^*$	vi; $\exists$Iφ
viii.	$\forall\varphi\Diamond A(\Theta, \varphi), w^*$	I, iv; $\Box$E
ix.	$\sim\exists\varphi\sim\Diamond A(\Theta, \varphi), w^*$	viii; Equiv.
x.	$\exists\varphi\sim\Diamond A(\Theta, \varphi) \wedge \sim\exists\varphi\sim\Diamond A(\Theta, \varphi), w^*$	vii, ix; $\wedge$I
xi.	$\bot$	x; LNC
xii.	$\sim\Diamond A(\Theta, (\sim\Diamond A(\Theta, p))), w$	A; per VE
xiii.	$\exists\varphi\sim\Diamond A(\Theta, \varphi), w$	xii; $\exists$Iφ
xiv.	$R(w, w)$	I; MR
xv.	$\forall\varphi\Diamond A(\Theta, \varphi), w$	i; MR
xvi.	$\sim\exists\varphi\sim\Diamond A(\Theta, \varphi), w$	xv; Equiv.
xvii.	$\exists\varphi\sim\Diamond A(\Theta, \varphi) \wedge \sim\exists\varphi\sim\Diamond A(\Theta, \varphi), w$	xiii, xvi; $\wedge$I
xviii.	$\bot$	xvii; LNC
xix.	$\bot$	ii, iii-xi, xii-xviii; VE

Having reached a contradiction in (xix), we might then denote ECQ, at which point the universe would explode.

N. B. Proof 1 may also be stated without needing to essentially index propositions to worlds. Sider's (2010: sect. 6.4) system, for example, could be used instead. In his system, the following schemata are valid and encoded as follows:

- (K*) $(\Box(p \supset q) \supset (\Box p \supset \Box q))$,
- (T) $(\Box p \supset p)$,
- (NEC) $(p \supset \Box p)$ (so long as "p" is a theorem of the logic).

To get the paradox underway, we then need only to first prove an important lemma:

- (Lemma) $(\Box(\forall\varphi\Diamond A(\alpha, \varphi) \supset \sim A(\alpha, \sim\Diamond A(\alpha, p))))$

The proof of this lemma runs as follows:

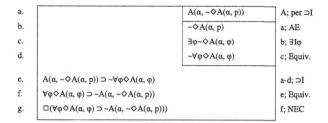

a.		A(α, ~◇A(α, p))	A; per ⊃I
b.		~◇A(α, p)	a; AE
c.		∃φ~◇A(α, φ)	b; ∃Iφ
d.		~∀φ◇A(α, φ)	c; Equiv.
e.	A(α, ~◇A(α, p)) ⊃ ~∀φ◇A(α, φ)		a-d; ⊃I
f.	∀φ◇A(α, φ) ⊃ ~A(α, ~◇A(α, p))		e; Equiv.
g.	□(∀φ◇A(α, φ) ⊃ ~A(α, ~◇A(α, p)))		f; NEC

With this lemma in hand, the stone paradox might then be formalized:

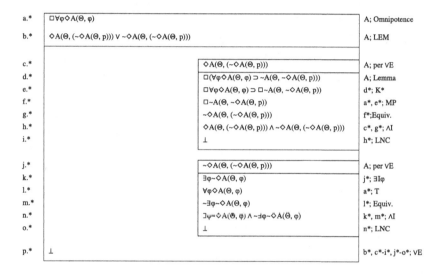

a.*	□∀φ◇A(Θ, φ)		A; Omnipotence
b.*	◇A(Θ, (~◇A(Θ, p))) ∨ ~◇A(Θ, (~◇A(Θ, p)))		A; LEM
c.*		◇A(Θ, (~◇A(Θ, p)))	A; per VE
d.*		□(∀φ◇A(Θ, φ) ⊃ ~A(Θ, ~◇A(Θ, p)))	A; Lemma
e.*		□∀φ◇A(Θ, φ) ⊃ □~A(Θ, ~◇A(Θ, p))	d*; K*
f.*		□~A(Θ, ~◇A(Θ, p))	a*, e*; MP
g.*		~◇A(Θ, (~◇A(Θ, p)))	f*;Equiv.
h.*		◇A(Θ, (~◇A(Θ, p))) ∧ ~◇A(Θ, (~◇A(Θ, p)))	c*, g*; AI
i.*		⊥	h*; LNC
j.*		~◇A(Θ, (~◇A(Θ, p)))	A; per VE
k.*		∃φ~◇A(Θ, φ)	j*; ∃Iφ
l.*		∀φ◇A(Θ, φ)	a*; T
m.*		~∃φ~◇A(Θ, φ)	l*; Equiv.
n.*		∃ψ~◇A(Θ, φ) ∧ ~∃φ~◇A(Θ, φ)	k*, m*; AI
o.*		⊥	n*; LNC
p.*	⊥		b*, c*-i*, j*-o*; VE

2 The Thomistic Solution

Let no one take offense at the saying, if we put limits even on the power of God. For to encompass things that are endless is by nature an impossibility. But when once the things, which God Himself grasps, have been bounded, necessity suffices as a boundary until the right number of things have been bounded.

(Origen of Alexandria c. 230/1966: *De Principiis*, bk. 4, ch. 4, sect. 8)

Limits Even on the Power of God

The Thomistic solution to the stone paradox targets premise (4) of our earlier informal statement of it:

4. If God cannot create the unliftable stone, then he is not omnipotent, since unable to create the stone.

The Thomists say that even though God cannot create an unliftable stone, this is no threat to classical theism. Omnipotence does not require that God can do absolutely anything, and creating such a stone is one among the things that omnipotence does not require being able to do. Were the extension of God's omnipotence given a more precise representation, no stone paradox would follow. This is by far the most popular response to omnipotence paradoxes. Notable representatives of the Thomistic tradition for revising the doctrine of omnipotence include: Origen (c. 230/1966), Pseudo-Dionysus (c. 500/1897), Anselm (1077/1975), Maimonides (1190/1956), Aquinas (1274/1952), Scotus (c. 1300/1987), Ockham (1318/1979), Malebranche (1688/1997), Lewis (1940/ 1962: ch. 2), Bittle (1953: ch. 13), Mayo (1961), Mavrodes (1963, 1977), Savage (1967), Plantinga (1967/1994: ch. 7), Londey and Miller (in Londey, Miller, & King-Farlow 1971), Schrader (1979), Rosenkrantz and Hoffman (1980, 1988), Flint and Freddoso (1983), Wierenga (1983), Wielenberg (2000), Leftow (2011), Świętorzecka (2011), Pearce and Pruss (2012), Pearce (2017, 2019), et al.

To this reply, the stone paradox proponent will immediately present two challenges. The first is to state precisely the ways in which divine omnipotence is restricted. And the second is to justify each of those restrictions. In place of (i), therefore, Thomists most usually offer an alternative analysis of omnipotence taking the form:

$$\Box\forall\varphi(\Diamond A(\Theta, \varphi) \equiv \Omega(\varphi)),$$

read as: "Necessarily, for all propositions, it is possible for God to actualize that proposition *just in case* its obtaining meets a specific set of conditions, Ω," which we can call the *omega conditions*. The omega conditions are usually presented as a long list of restrictions, which seems to grow from author to author. Morriston (2002: 358) complains: "In recent years, definitions of omnipotence have become more and more complicated. Indeed, they frequently employ so much technical apparatus and contain so many subordinate clauses and qualifications, that it is natural to wonder whether they have much to do with what an ordinary person might mean by saying that God is all-powerful." But the Thomists' list can be simplified. Proposed omega conditions divide into three categories. First, Thomists say that omnipotence does not require doing the *logically impossible*. So, it is no threat to God's omnipotence to be unable to square a circle or climb an actually infinite staircase or correctly calculate that $2 + 2 = 5$ or otherwise actualize a jointly inconsistent set of propositions, and so on. This knocks out some stone paradoxes, but not all of them. Notably, it does not resolve the canonical version of the stone paradox, since being able to create an object too heavy for oneself to lift is a logically contingent predicate that is in fact true of most of us (cf. Mavrodes 1963).

The second omega condition attempts to address the remainder of the stone paradoxes. Thomists say that omnipotence does not require doing the *essentially impossible*, by which is meant doing something that would contradict the specific omnipotent being's essence. So, it is no threat to God's omnipotence to be unable to make things that he can't subsequently control or make rules that bind himself or *deny himself* and his own omnipotence, because he is *essentially omnipotent*. This knocks out the rest of the stone paradoxes. Additionally, this constraint helps Thomists resolve several type-B omnipotence paradoxes. For example, it would follow that it is no threat to God's omnipotence to be unable to get a B+ on a logic exam, since essentially impeccable; to be unable to deceive, since essentially omnibenevolent; or to be unable to pose himself a riddle so difficult that even he can't resolve it, since essentially omniscient; and so on.

It is worth pausing to further extol the virtues of this last feature of the Thomistic solution. Earlier, I said that the most rational way to resolve a good paradox is to follow Quine's maxim of minimum mutilation. But it would seem that our method of rational paradox resolution is incomplete. The analytic classical theist faces not one paradox, but rather a host of them; and when facing multiple paradoxes at once, all involving a common stock of beliefs, additional resources for rational paradox resolution become available. Contemporary abductive logicians recommend we evaluate competing hypotheses according to each proposal's comparative *theoretical virtues*. A theoretical virtue is a feature of a hypothesis that makes it, all things being equal, a better theory. There are many documented theoretical virtues, such as simplicity (Ockham's razor), conservatism, testability, durability, fruitfulness, scope, elegance, and so on. (cf. Vaughn 2016: chs. 9–10; Keas 2018). A proposed solution to a paradox is a kind of hypothesis, too: It is a *diagnosis* of what has gone wrong in an agent's belief. Consequently, we might evaluate competing solutions to paradoxes in ways analogous to how we evaluate competing hypotheses. The Thomistic solution, in its potential for resolving several theological paradoxes all at once, would seem to have a theoretical virtue of *scope*, since rather than requiring that the analytic theist tackle each omnipotence paradox singly, it proposes one method by which they might resolve many. Again, if a person's noetic structure may be likened to a great web, and a single paradox may be likened to a knot in their web, then several paradoxes surrounding the same stock of beliefs may be likened to a tangled mess. If the Thomist, by revising the doctrine of divine omnipotence, can pull just a single thread and thereby untangle multiple knots at once, this is prima facie a mark in favor of their solution.

Third, Thomists say that omnipotence does not require doing the *metaphysically impossible*. In particular, Thomists say it is no threat to God's power to be unable to change the past or contravene human free will. Of the three classes of omega restrictions, this third is the least well motivated. But the dialectical reason for their addition is clear. We noted earlier that free will plays a major role in popular theodicies, especially in replies to paradoxes of evil. But if God could violate free will, then it could no longer serve as a solution to those paradoxes (cf. Conee 1991: sect. 6). Moreover, if God could alter the past, then revealed theologians worry that God could nullify his past covenants with humanity without violating them – namely, by changing the past situations in which they were initially established (cf. Molina 1588/1988: disp. 51, sect. 19). So, for the sake of *universal coherence* within the analytic theist's other responses to theological paradoxes, as well as within revealed Abrahamic theology, they must assume that God's omnipotence is limited in these ways, too.

In summary, the Thomist contends that God can actualize any proposition if and only if that proposition meets the omega conditions, where the omega conditions are defined:

$$\Box \forall \varphi (\Diamond A(\Theta, \varphi) \equiv \Omega(\varphi) \equiv (L(\varphi) \wedge E(\varphi, \Theta) \wedge M(\varphi))),$$

that is, the proposition's obtaining is consistent with the laws of logic, consistent with God's essence, and consistent with the laws of metaphysics. My stone paradox riddler raises the question:

$$\Diamond A(\Theta, (\sim \Diamond A(\Theta, p)))?$$

The Thomist says the correct answer is that God *cannot* do such a thing, since to do so would violate logic and his own essential omnipotence. But, being essentially omnipotent, God's omnipotence does not require that he be able to do this anyway, per the first and second omega conditions.

Why might one think these omega restrictions are warranted? And are these restrictions overall plausible given an intuitive understanding of what an omnipotent agent should be able to do? In this section, I'll survey Thomistic arguments for the omega restrictions. I'll focus on the first two, since the third is not as relevant to the debate surrounding the stone paradox. My dialectical stance here is generally oppositional. Some of the Thomists' arguments are prima facie plausible, while some are not, and so I'll first criticize certain motivations for the omega restrictions. Then I'll turn to examining the account on its own right, and

I'll rehearse counterarguments to the effect that restricting God's power in these ways would lead to strongly counterintuitive consequences.

Absolute Impossibility

Thomists say that God's omnipotence does not require being able to actualize logical contradictions. (Some say that God cannot actualize logical tautologies either – cf., e.g., Wierenga 1983: 365; but cf. also Schrader 1979: 257ff.) Why might one think that God cannot do the logically impossible? Two arguments suggest themselves. First, the Thomist may point out that we do not *ordinarily* consider the inability to do the logically impossible as limitations on an agent's genuine ability. For example, a skilled feline veterinarian who can claim to be able to provide medical assistance to any cat need not be able to treat a Cheshire cat, a cat that is both present and absent at once, thus violating the LNC (cf. Carroll 1897). Similarly, it is no threat to a master mathematician's mathematical prowess that they cannot divide a quantity by zero. By the same token, we therefore ought not suppose that the divine agent must be able to break laws of logic either (cf. Frankfurt 1977: 43; cf. also Conee 1991: 452–453). But this argument is not very convincing, since it is susceptible to the accusation of anthropomorphism. It is in general inappropriate to reason from how we speak of human agents to how we should speak of God. We would, for example, excuse the vet if they could not resurrect a dead cat, but an omnipotent being should be able to do this. Just so, we would excuse the mathematician from calculating the decimals of the number π to the duotrigintillionth place, since life is short; but again, the divine mathematician should be able to do this too. Similarly, a critic could say, even if we excuse human agents from doing the impossible, we should not so excuse an omnipotent being.

So, second, the Thomist may follow the lead of Aquinas. On this point, St. Thomas (1274/1952) reasons:

> [A] thing is said to be possible or impossible absolutely according to the relation in which the very terms stand to one another: possible if the predicate is not incompatible with the subject, as that Socrates sits; and absolutely impossible when the predicate is altogether incompatible with the subject, as, for instance, that a man is a donkey. .... Therefore, everything that does not imply a contradiction is numbered amongst those possible things, in respect of which God is called omnipotent; but whatever implies a contradiction does not come within the scope of divine omnipotence, because it cannot have the aspect of possibility. Hence it is better to say that such things cannot be done, than that God cannot do them. ... For whatever implies a contradiction cannot be a word, because no intellect can possibly conceive such a thing. (ST, pt. 1, Q25, A3)

There are some difficulties with this passage, but they are easily amendable. A critic may complain that Aquinas's conception of logical impossibility is what would be better described as *analytical* impossibility, since the impossibility is dependent on the meaning of the terms rather than on the logical syntax of the proposition (cf. Quine 1951/2003). But presumably Aquinas would agree that a proposition of the form "A man is not a man" is also absolutely impossible. And so, the modern Thomist could restrict the argument's scope just to propositions of that sort. Additionally, some critics of Aquinas have focused their attention on his claim that a contradictory proposition "cannot be a word," by which presumably he means a genuine proposition. For this reason, Geach complains that St. Thomas has mistakenly assumed that illogical propositions are nonsensical, which, as noted earlier, is false. Geach (1973: 13): "Aquinas, writing seven centuries ago, is excusable for not being clear about the difference between self-contradiction and gibberish; we are not excusable if we are not" (cf. also Clark 2017: 256–258).

But this is uncharitable, since Aquinas immediately goes on to say why he really thinks logical impossibilities are outside of the scope of divine omnipotence: "[B]ecause no intellect can possibly conceive such a thing." If we instead focus our attention on this claim, then I think we can understand Aquinas's argument here as an enthymemic syllogism in which the major premise is suppressed (cf. Leftow 2012). Malebranche (1688/1997: dialogue 3) would seem to offer the same argument, in fact, but in which the minor is suppressed. Malebranche reasons that, "God can do whatever He sees and whatever He makes us see clearly and distinct in His light." From which he infers, "He can do anything that does not involve a contradiction." Accordingly, I propose that Aquinas's argument, stated more explicitly, runs:

[Major]   No inconceivable proposition is actualizable by an omnipotent being.
[Minor]   All logically contradictory propositions are inconceivable.
[Conclusion] No logically contradictory proposition is actualizable by an omnipotent being.

This argument is prima facie plausible. It is deductively valid, taking a classical syllogistic EAE-1 form, and both premises seem true. But if the premises are not intuitively obvious to the reader, supporting arguments may be offered.

In support of the major: Indeed, how else could God actualize a proposition other than by than initially conceiving of what it is he means to actualize?

A critic may perhaps raise the possibility that God might *unintentionally* actualize a proposition, which does not require first conceiving it. But the Thomist has a reply to this putative counterexample: The ability to unintentionally actualize a proposition would seem to be irrelevant to omnipotence. Rather, what we mean in saying that God is omnipotent is that "He can do from Himself and through Himself whatever He *wills* to do" (William of Auxerre [c. 1215]: *Summa Aurea*; in Leftow 2011). So, if the critic would have us restrict the type of actualization under discussion to intentional actualization, then we may do so, *salva veritate*.

And the minor may be supported in two ways. The first way is phenomenological. Introspection reveals that we cannot conceive of what it would mean for a logically contradictory proposition to be true. Even a committed dialetheist could concede this point, too. Descartes (1629–1649/1970), for instance, writes: "[God] has given me such a mind that I cannot conceive a mountain without a valley, or an aggregate of one and two which is not three ... [S]uch things involve a contradiction in my conception" [Letter to Arnauld, 29 July 1648]. And the second way is through an analysis of conceptual content. For example, Lewis (1986/2005: ch. 1, sect. 4) proposes a possible worlds analysis of conceptual content, according to which, in an act of conceptualization, what we directly apprehend are sets of possible worlds. (Note that this theory is controversial; but its limitations are inconsequential to the following point, for which it would seem to be adequate – cf. Heck 2012.) The total domain of possible worlds is defined by what is logically possible. For suppose that there were impossible worlds in logical space. In that case, there would be a world at which a contradiction is true. But if a contradiction were true at one world, then, by appealing to ECQ, we could deduce that every contradiction must be true at every other world, too. For if a contraction entails anything, then the following inferential pattern is valid (assuming minimal modal assumptions – a modal version of ECQ, ECQ□; NEC; a variant of K*, K◇; and then B, modal symmetry):

$$\Diamond(p \wedge \sim p) \vdash \Box(p \wedge \sim p)$$

The modal schemata needed are (cf. Sider 2010: sect. 6.4):

- (ECQ□) $((p \wedge \sim p) \supset \Box q)$,
- (NEC) $(p \supset \Box p)$ (if "p" is a theorem),
- (K◇) $(\Box(p \supset q) \supset (\Diamond p \supset \Diamond q))$,
- (B) $(\Diamond \Box p \supset p)$.

The proof then runs as follows:

a.**	$\Diamond(p \wedge \sim p)$	Assumption
b.**	$(p \wedge \sim p) \supset \Box(p \wedge \sim p)$	ECQ□
c.**	$\Box((p \wedge \sim p) \supset \Box(p \wedge \sim p))$	b**; NEC
d.**	$(\Box((p \wedge \sim p) \supset \Box(p \wedge \sim p))) \supset (\Diamond(p \wedge \sim p) \supset \Diamond\Box(p \wedge \sim p))$	K$\Diamond$
e.**	$\Diamond(p \wedge \sim p) \supset \Diamond\Box(p \wedge \sim p)$	c**, d**; MP
f.**	$\Diamond\Box(p \wedge \sim p)$	a**, e**; MP
g.**	$\Diamond\Box(p \wedge \sim p) \supset (p \wedge \sim p)$	B
h.**	$(p \wedge \sim p)$	f**, g**; MP
i.**	$\Box(p \wedge \sim p)$	b**, h**; MP

(N.B. (i**) could also be deduced from (f**) with the S5 schema ($\Diamond\Box p \supset \Box p$), instead of B.) But this is absurd. It would entail, among other things, that we cannot actually conceive of distinct possibilities, when clearly we can. Therefore, since there are no possible worlds at which a contradiction is true, and conceptual content is defined in terms of possible worlds, no contradiction can be conceived either (cf. Sainsbury 2008: ch. 9).

Ability and Liability

Thomists say that God's omnipotence does not require being able to act against his own essence. Why might one think this? Again, two arguments suggest themselves. First, the Thomist may argue from the nature of essence. An old adage of scholastic philosophical cosmology has it that, in general, no essence of a thing is capable of destroying itself or its bearer. Essential destruction must therefore always arise as a result of something nonidentical to a thing (*quidquid movetur, ab alio movetur*) (cf. Aristotle c. 350 BC/ 1941c: *Physics*; bk. 8, ch. 4, inter alia; Aquinas 1265: SCG, bk. 1, ch. 5, sects. 5–10; Bittle 1939: ch. 9). But every attribute God possesses he possesses essentially, including his omnipotence; what's more, in his perfect simplicity, he *just is* his essence; and no agent could possibly overpower an omnipotent being: "[N]othing is held to be done against God's will, which is himself, in such a way that what he wills to be done is not done, or what he does not will to be done is done" (Lombard c. 1155/2007: bk. 1, disp. 42). Therefore, it is no limitation on God's omnipotence that he cannot do anything opposed to his own essence. This argument, however, is unsound. The scholastic *quidquid movetur* principle cannot be maintained in light of contemporary physical science. We know now that it does belong to the essence of certain substances to self-corrupt – the *radioactive elements* (like uranium), for example (cf. Bittle 1941: 332–333). Consequently, a critic may argue that, if uranium, and so on, can spontaneously corrupt their own essences and *transmutate*, then perhaps God's essential omnipotence is radioactive, too (Serway & Vuille 2015: ch. 29).

Instead of arguing from the nature of essence, the Thomist may follow the lead of Boethius (524/1999: bk. 4, ch. 2), Anselm (1077/1975: ch. 7), Aquinas (1274/1952: ST, pt. 1, Q25, A3), et al. They were concerned to show in particular that God cannot sin, which would contradict his own essential omnibenevolence (cf. Aristotle c. 350 BCb: *Topics*, ch. 4, 126a 34). But the argument they offer would seem to be entirely generalizable to other cases of God potentially thwarting his own essence, as well. Their arguments, put one way or another, depend on a distinction between agential *ability*, on the one hand, and agential *liability*, on the other (cf. Morriston 2002: 365ff). "Ability" is a term of success, such that to have an ability is to have the power or strength to accomplish some task. "Liability" is a term of unsuccess, such that to have a liability is to have a weakness, to be able to fail at some task or "fall short of action," as St. Thomas puts it. With this distinction in hand, one of two argumentative strategies might be employed.

First, the Thomist could show that, *in every particular case*, to be able to be impersonal, corporeal, unfree, mistaken, ignorant, malevolent, peccable, passable, fallible, contingent, impotent – and so on for the other divine attributes – are all banes, not boons. But in saying God is "omnipotent," we mean only to say that he has every power, not every weakness as well. Swinburne (1994: 129): "God is omnipotent in that whatever he chooses to do, he *succeeds* in doing." Consequently, God cannot thwart any of his own essential attributes. Or, second, and more directly, the Thomist could show that, *in general*, to be able to thwart one's own essential nature is no genuine ability, but likewise only a liability. Again, in saying God is omnipotent, we mean only to say he has every ability, not every liability, too. If the critic insists, the Thomist might modify their definition of omnipotence, *salva veritate*, in order to stipulate that the only propositions under the scope of the universal propositional operator express agential abilities (cf. Aquinas 1265: SCG, bk. 2, ch. 25).

Making What's Done Undone

The third omega condition is not directly related to the Thomistic solution to the stone paradox, but it is worth briefly discussing anyway, since it is of pedagogical value and will be useful later. Most Thomists say that God's omnipotence does not require being able to violate the laws of metaphysics, such as making it the case that "existence should become identical with nothing" (Averroes c. 1150/1969: ch. 2) or that "the elementary components of a thing, substance and accident, . . . interchange, so that the substance becomes accident, and the accident becomes substance" (Maimonides 1190/1956: pt. 3, ch. 15). However, other Thomists say merely that God cannot actualize *certain* metaphysical impossibilities, since they may wish to maintain at once, say, that the ENN is a legitimate metaphysical law but also that God created everything ex nihilo; and they wish also to allow for other metaphysical miracles.

Most commonly, Thomists specify that, minimally, God cannot change the past, such that what was done is undone (cf. Aristotle c. 350 BC/1941b: *Ethics*, bk. 6, ch. 2. 1139b 5–11); and he cannot make it the case that a free agent freely does some action, since then it would not have been done *freely* (cf. Flint & Freddoso 1983; Rosenkrantz & Hoffman 1980b). Just as Molinists say that God possesses only middle knowledge of free human action, Thomists who are sympathetic with this latter omega restriction might say that God possesses only *middle power* (*potentia media*) with respect to free human action: God cannot make it the case that I freely perform some action, but he can make it the case that some conditions obtain such that, were those conditions to obtain, then I would freely perform that action. I will not discuss at any length arguments against God's contravening human free will, since this would mean discussing the debate between libertarianism and compatibilism, which would take us too far afield (cf. Young 1976; Thai & Pillay 2020). But I will briefly consider further God's inability to change the past.

Why might one think that God cannot change the past? On this point, many Thomists express the intuition that, albeit metaphysically contingent, past events are nonetheless temporally fixed relative to the present (cf. Prior 1955). Aquinas reasons that this fact is baked into our temporal language, so that to even speak of changing the past is contradictory. St. Thomas (1274/1952) writes:

> [T]hat the past should not have been implies a contradiction. For as it implies a contradiction to say that Socrates is sitting, and is not sitting, so does it to say that he sat, and did not sit. But to say that he did sit is to say that it happened in the past. To say that he did not sit, is to say that it did not happen. Hence, that the past should not have been does not come under the scope of divine power. (ST, pt. 1, Q25, A4)

The Thomistic argument against God's potentially changing the past is problematic. This is so for three reasons. First, Aquinas's argument, taken one way, would seem to prove too little. Leftow (2012): "Granted, if God does not remove Socrates's sitting from the past, we get a contradiction. But why couldn't God remove this? That is, why could he not make it the case simply that Socrates *never* sat – that it has never been the case that Socrates did anything other than not sit? Aquinas does not say."

Second, Aquinas's argument, taken another way, would seem to prove too much. If Aquinas's argument is sound, then it would follow that not only can

God not affect the past, but neither can he change the present or the future; which is absurd. St. Peter Damian (1065/1969: 149–150) reasons:

> For truly, whatever exists at the moment, so long as it exists, must undoubtedly exist. For it is not true that so long as something exists, it is possible for it not to exist. In like manner, for something that will happen, it is impossible for it not to happen, even though there may be some things whose happening or not happening is a matter of indifference, as, for example, . . . our having rain or clear weather. . . . [B]ut these are called "indifferent alternatives" more properly in relation to the variable nature of things than to the logical consequence of speech. . . . [B]y the logic of words, if it is going to rain, it is absolutely necessary that it rain. Likewise, what is said of past events may be applied with equal cogency to present and future things. . . . And so in relation to the logical order of speech, for whatever was, it is impossible not to have been; for whatever is, it is impossible not to be; and for whatever will be, it is impossible that it will not be.

Finally, classical theists say that God is *omnitemporal*, but there are at least two interpretations of this divine attribute (cf. Craig 2011). The preceding Thomistic argument assumes that this must mean that God is *sempiternal*. Sempiternity is the state of being present in every moment of time, from one changing moment to the next. A sempiternal being therefore acts from within time. Damian (1065/1969), however, holds that God's omnitemporality is better understood as meaning that he is *eternal*. Eternality is the state of being outside of time but nonetheless existing from the perspective of every moment in time. An eternal being therefore does not act from within time but, acting timelessly, nonetheless might affect any moment in time, past, present, or future (cf. Remnant 1978; Holopainen 2020). St. Peter's interpretation is superior to St. Thomas's. One argument for this runs as follows. God is perfectly essential – that is, he possesses every property he possesses essentially. But if God is in time and bears a relation to objects in time (such as caring for them, as Abrahamic theists maintain), then the properties that God possesses must change over time, such as when those objects cease to exist. But a thing's essence cannot change over time. Consequently, God cannot exist in time (cf. Bassford 2021). Therefore, he must be eternal, not sempiternal (cf. Aquinas 1274/1952: ST, pt. 1, Q10; Q14, A13; Q57, A3). If so, then God might freely change the past, present, or future without contradiction.

The Case of Mr. McEar

Let's take stock. The Thomist contends that God's omnipotence does not require that he be able to violate laws of logic, his own essence, or (at least certain) laws of metaphysics, such as making what's done undone. So far, I've been offering a critical survey of Thomistic motivations for these restrictions. The best argument for the first omega condition is that logical contradictions are inconceivable, and an omnipotent being need only to be able to actualize conceivable propositions. The best argument for the second is that violating one's own essence is a liability, not an ability, and an omnipotent being need only to be able to actualize propositions expressing genuine abilities. Finally, St. Thomas argues that an omnipotent being cannot change the past, since this would be contradictory, too; but we found the argument for this restriction wanting. (The third omega condition, however, is strictly irrelevant to the Thomistic solution to the stone paradox, and so we can leave it aside moving forward.) I turn now from critique to counterargument. I raise the question: Is the Thomistic account of God's omnipotence plausible, given reasonable intuitions about what an omnipotent being should be able to do? I answer that it is not. To demonstrate that this is so, I will rehearse two popular objections to the account: *The Case of Mr. McEar* and *A Divine Tug-of-War*.

The case of Mr. McEar traces its roots back to Ockham (1318/1979), if not earlier. In the contemporary literature, it was first introduced by Plantinga (1967/1994: 168–173); McEar was then baptized by La Croix (1975: 253ff; 1977: 183). The case runs as follows. McEar is a being who is essentially such that he is capable only of scratching his left ear (as well as any action that is required to do so – cf. Leftow 2011). Moreover, he is such that he only ever wills to scratch his left ear, if he wills for anything. He is, however, perfectly effective at doing so, such that anytime he wills to scratch his left ear, he succeeds. A being who can only scratch his left ear, no matter how effective he is at doing so, is clearly not an omnipotent being. Ockham (1318/1979: *Ordinatio*, pt. 1, dist. 42): "Nor is a being said to be omnipotent because he can do all things which are possible *for him* to do … since it would follow that a minimally powerful being is omnipotent." But the problem is that, on the Thomist definition of omnipotence, it should follow that McEar is in fact omnipotent; which is absurd. This is because McEar is such that he can possibly actualize any proposition that is logically possible and consistent with his essence, and as the Thomist says, to thwart one's own essence – in this case by McEar's doing something other than scratching his left ear – is no restriction on an omnipotent being. Consequently, if God is omnipotent, though unable to create a stone too heavy for him to lift, so too is McEar, though hardly able to do anything at all.

In response, the Thomist might say that this reductio just goes to show that McEar is a mere *impossibilium*, that there could be no such essentially impotent being (cf. Wierenga 1983: 374–375; 1989). But this defense cannot be maintained, since God could presumably create such a being. The Thomist should say so too, since creating McEar would violate none of the omega conditions on God's power. Still, the Thomist might appeal to omnipotence here to support the opposite contention: As omnipotent, God could always give McEar more power than he has, and it is for this reason that McEar is impossible. But this defense cannot be maintained either. First, to give McEar more power would violate McEar's essence. So, God's giving him more power is metaphysically impossible, which violates the third omega condition. Second, if God can modify McEar's essence, then we might well ask: Why could God not then also modify his own essence – say, to allow him to create a stone too heavy for him to lift?

Alternatively, the Thomist might say that this reductio just goes to show that, per contra, McEar *is* omnipotent. To support this reply, the Thomist might again appeal to the ability–liability distinction. Indeed, given that McEar is essentially constituted to only be able to scratch his left ear, to do anything else would thwart his essence and thus would be a liability for him, not a genuine ability. This reply, however, is counterintuitive. For consider that Tony Hawk's power to perform a triple kickflip on a skateboard is intuitively a great ability; but this reply would have it that, per impossibile, were McEar to perform a triple kickflip, this would be no great ability at all.

Still, the Thomist might say that this reply is not so counterintuitive; moreover, my critique in the preceding paragraph depends on thinking of abilities and liabilities as absolute, but this distinction is better understood as being always species-relative (cf. Clark 2017: 253–255). For consider that, if I cannot see, then we would say that I lack a natural ability; but if a bat cannot see, we would not say that the bat lacks an ability, since bats are naturally sightless. St. Thomas contends that, in general, a thing's power is an ability for it just in case, in exercising it, the being thereby perfects itself and its essence; whereas, a power is a liability for a thing just in case, in exercising it, the being thereby imperfects itself and its essence (cf. Aquinas 1272: *In Met.*, bk. 9, ch. 8). This is a teleological account of abilities, in that every genuine ability of a thing is directed to some end, the end of actualizing a being's native potential (cf. Aquinas 1271: *In Phys.*, bk. 3, ch. 1). Now consider my power to blind myself. On Aquinas's account, this comes out as a liability, since exercising this power would destroy my vision, which is natural to my specific essence (cf. Aquinas c. 1255/2014). Applied to McEar, then, given that his essence is such that scratching his left ear is the sole natural potential of his species, to exercise this power is an ability for him, whereas to do otherwise would imperfect him and his specific essence, akin to my blinding myself. Again, omnipotence should be understood only in terms of abilities, not liabilities. Consequently, we should conclude that McEar is omnipotent after all.

But this argument is not plausible, because it is false that the ability–liability distinction is confined to specific essences. We can also compare the abilities of different species, as well as individual members of different species, and pass judgment on whose abilities are greater. A thought experiment helps to illustrate this (cf. Wielenberg 2000: 29–31). Suppose that Mr. McEar is married to Mrs. McEar, and they have two children, McEar Jr. and Missy McEar. Mr. McEar, as we said, can scratch only his left ear; Mrs. McEar can scratch both her left and right ears; and they're very proud of their children, for Junior can scratch both ears and his chin, and Missy can scratch her ears, her chin, and her nose. Intuitively, Missy is more powerful than Junior, who is more powerful than Missus, who is in turn more powerful than Mister. And this is so despite their each having different specific essences. Now, on the Thomist definition of omnipotence, all four McEars are equally omnipotent. But no one can be more powerful than an omnipotent being, since "omnipotent" is surely a superlative term, not admitting of there being agents who are more omnipotent than others. Consequently, the Thomistic defense of McEar's omnipotence cannot be maintained.

Finally, the Thomist might accept the reductio against the Thomistic definition of omnipotence, but they might say that this just goes to show that the account needs revision. Pearce and Pruss (2012) take this tack and suggest that the reason that McEar is not actually omnipotent is because he lacks *freedom of will*, which they think is a necessary condition on omnipotence. Not only can McEar only scratch his left ear, but as we said, he can only *will* that, too; but surely an omnipotent being should be able to will more than just that. Accordingly, Pearce and Pruss abandon the omega conditions and instead offer this definition: God is omnipotent just in case he has perfect *efficacy of will* and perfect *freedom of will* too (405) (cf. also Pearce 2017, 2019). McEar has perfect efficacy of will but he obviously does not have perfect freedom of will, since there is much he cannot will.

Pearce and Pruss (2012) contend that this definition correctly (and conservatively) identifies the range of God's power. Even a perfectly free will cannot will certain propositions. However, whereas some limitations on free will are *mere limitations*, others are *constraints*. A constraint diminishes an agent's free will; a (mere) limitation does not (410). Pearce and Pruss then contend that perfect free will entails that the willer possess several other attributes, which all limit without constraining what he can will: omniscience, omnibenevolence, impeccability … and all of the other divine attributes, as well (411ff). So, Pearce and Pruss agree with the Thomist that God cannot create a stone too heavy for him to lift, but they disagree with the traditional account as to why he cannot do so. Per his efficacy of will, he might create such a stone;

but per his freedom of will, he could never *will* to do so (but cf. 407–408). (This distinction is similar to the classical theological distinction between God's *potentia absoluta* and his *potentia ordinata* – cf. Geach 1973: 16; Alanen 1988: 184.)

This alternative analysis of omnipotence, however, is not very plausible either. Pearce and Pruss contend that omnipotence entails the other divine attributes, but as a matter of *conceptual* analysis, this would seem to be false (cf. Morriston 2001: 9–10). Descartes (1641/2006) famously offered a case of an omnipotent being who is not omnibenevolent – his infamous *evil demon*. We can conceive of such a being without contradiction. But if Pearce and Pruss's conceptual analysis were correct, Descartes's evil demon is logically impossible. Similarly, we can conceive of an omnipotent being who lacks omniscience without contradiction – a sort of superpowered *Hercules*, for example. (Hercules could make himself omniscient, but he never actually does.) A being like Hercules, lacking foresight, very well might will to create a stone too heavy for him to lift. Classical theists agree that all of the divine attributes are metaphysically identical to one another and God; but conceptually, logically, they are distinct. And so, even if Pearce and Pruss's alternative analysis would resolve the McEar objection, it would seem not to resolve the stone paradox or certain other omnipotence paradoxes; which was the primary objective of the analysis.

A Divine Tug-of-War

The divine tug-of-war objection is sometimes called "the new stone paradox" (cf. Mele & Smith 1988; cf. also Wielenberg 2001), but it has medieval origins, going back at least to Al-Ghazali (1096/1965, ch. 5) and Scotus (c. 1300/1987: bk. 1, dist. 2, Q3). Like the original stone paradox, the best prosaic presentation of the new stone paradox takes an interrogative form, this time unfolding over a series of three questions. First question: Can God create another essentially omnipotent being? Presumably the answer here is that he can. After all, creating another omnipotent being contradicts neither logic nor God's essence. And so, suppose God exercises his power and creates a second essentially omnipotent being, Titan. Second question: Could God and Titan agree to a friendly tug-of-war? Again, presumably the answer here is that they could. After all, they are both omnipotent, and agreeing to a tug-of-war would butt up against neither logic nor their own essences. And so, suppose God and Titan pick up the rope. Final question: Who would win the contest – God or Titan? The Thomist faces a destructive quadrilemma: Either God would win, Titan would win, both would win, or neither would win the war. All four responses would lead to some or another absurd result.

The Thomist cannot say that *God* would win, since Titan is omnipotent, and, as we said, no one can thwart an omnipotent being if that being does not wish to be thwarted. By the same token, they cannot say that *Titan* would win either: "For God is ... mighty in strength. Who [could] ever challenge him and succeed?" (Job 9:4). They cannot say that *both* would win. If God wins, then the rope has moved closer to him. If Titan wins, then the rope has not moved closer to God. Consequently, if both would win, we would have to say that the rope would both move and not move closer to God at one and the same time, which is absurd. So, the Thomist should say that *neither* would win; that way there is no contradiction of either logic or essence. In fact, if an omnipotent being's inability to create an unliftable stone is no threat to their power, then, just so, the inability to win a divine tug-of-war should be no threat to their power either.

However, two counterintuitive consequences would follow from this response. First, if the Thomist contends that no omnipotent being can win a contest against any other, then it should not matter how many omnipotent beings are pitted up against one another. But suppose, fearing his defeat, Titan were to create ninety-eight more omnipotent beings to help him in the war. So now God is pulling on one end of the rope, and ninety-nine titans are pulling on the other. The Thomist would have to say that, even in this case, neither party would win the war. But, more intuitively, the titans would win it (cf. Werner 1971: 67). Second, if the Thomist contends that no omnipotent being can win a contest against any other, then it would follow that it is possible for a being to be omnipotent even though he cannot do anything whatsoever. For suppose that Titan is pugnacious, and he decides to contest God in *everything* that God might do. For example, God wills to lift a perfectly liftable stone, but Titan then wills that God does not lift the stone. It would follow that God cannot possibly succeed, even though he is omnipotent. But this is counterintuitive, too; surely no being is omnipotent who cannot successfully actualize even a single proposition (cf. Baillie & Hagen 2008: 32–33).

In response, the Thomist might say that this reductio just goes to show that God cannot create another omnipotent being. To support this contention, they might argue that God's creating a second omnipotent being would violate a law of logic. But this defense cannot be maintained, since the fourth horn in this quadrilemma leads to no logical contradiction but simply a counterintuitive reply with respect to Thomistic omnipotence, which is the point. So, the Thomist might argue instead that God's creating a second omnipotent being would violate his own essence. But this defense cannot be maintained either. This can be illustrated by considering other scenarios in which God might create a second omnipotent being and no counterintuitive consequences follow. For example, perhaps Titan is an amiable omnipotent being such that, whatever God wills to do, Titan supports it and in no way ever opposes God. (Titan could oppose God, but he never actually does.) In this scenario, there could be two omnipotent beings at a world and God's essence would not be contradicted (cf. De Florio & Frigerio 2015: 317ff). Alternatively, the Thomist might say that this reductio just goes to show that two omnipotent beings could not challenge one another to a tug-of-war. But if the Thomist takes this line, then they face an explanatory challenge. What exactly about the divine tug-of-war is supposed to be contradictory: issuing the challenge, picking up the rope, pulling on the rope? None of these actions is logically contradictory, and intuitively, none of these actions would seem opposed to God's essential omnipotence. More to the point, an omnipotent being should be able to perform them all.

So, finally, the Thomist might reply that the paradox issues a false quadrilemma. I have said that one, the other, both, or neither contestants must win the war. But there are other possibilities. For example, perhaps the rope simply ceases to exist. This, however, is not a genuinely distinct possibility, since this option reduces to the fourth. Neither contestant will have won the war if the rope is annihilated, since a condition on winning a tug-of-war is pulling the rope over to one's side, and one cannot do that if there is no longer any rope to pull (cf. Baillie & Hagen 2008: 25). The divine tug-of-war objection, therefore, demonstrates not that the Thomistic re-definition of omnipotence is incoherent but only that its proposed omega restrictions entail some strongly counterintuitive consequences, given reasonable, pre-theoretical intuitions about omnipotence.

Let's review. The Thomist's re-definition of omnipotence faces two popular counterarguments. The first is the case of Mr. McEar, which argues that, if being unable to act contrary to one's own essence is no threat to an agent's being omnipotent, then it should follow that McEar is omnipotent, too, even though he can only scratch his left ear. But this is absurd. And the second is the new stone paradox, which argues that, if the Thomist's definition is correct, then God should also be able to create another essentially omnipotent being. But if he could, then it would follow that God might still be omnipotent, even if he can't do anything at all, which is absurd, too. For these reasons, the Thomist solution to the stone paradox is not a perfect resolution of it, in accordance with our maxim of minimum mutilation. For even if it would successfully untangle one knot in the analytic theist's doxastic web, it would do so at the cost of creating knots elsewhere.

3 The Cartesian Solution

> Hence, if God happens to reveal to us something about himself or others which is
> beyond the natural reach of the mind[,] . . . we will not refuse to believe it, despite
> the fact that we do not clearly understand it. And we will not be at all surprised
> that there is much, both in the immeasurable nature of God and in the things
> created by him, which is beyond our mental capacity.
>
> (Descartes 1647/1996: *Principles of Philosophy*, pt. 1, sect. 25)

No Limits on the Power of God

The Cartesian solution to the stone paradox targets premise (3) of our earlier
informal statement of it:

3. If God can create the unliftable stone, then he is not omnipotent, since unable
   to lift the stone.

The Cartesians say that, if God were to create an unliftable stone, he might
still lift it. Omnipotence permits that God can do absolutely anything, even
the superlogical. Consequently, Cartesians would seem to target line (xi) of
our formal presentation on the paradox, the putative absurdity arising from
the dilemma's first horn. (Alternatively, they might target line (viii) – more
on this shortly.) Cartesianism is a form of *weak dialetheism*, according to
which some contradictions are possibly true. The scenario in which God
creates an unliftable stone and then lifts it is just one such contradictory
scenario. And in possible scenarios in which a contradiction obtains, the
law of noncontradiction fails: $(p \wedge \sim p) \not\vdash \bot$; as does *explosion*: $(p \wedge \sim p) \not\vdash$
q. This is not a very popular response to omnipotence paradoxes. Notable
representatives of the Cartesian tradition for revising classical logic are
few: Descartes (1629–1649/1970, 1641/2006, 1647/1996), Frankfurt
(1964), and Conee (1991).

  The Cartesian solution has traditionally been greeted in the literature with one
of two dismissive responses. Some dismiss it as being too naïve to take
seriously. In this spirit, Geach (1973: 10) writes that Cartesianism is
a position that only a college freshman would find plausible; and Leftow
(2011) accordingly calls this the "frosh" solution to the paradox. Others dismiss
it as being too absurd to take seriously. In this spirit, Anderson (1984: 111)
writes:

> Frankfurt [1964] suggests ... If we allow that God can do the self-
> contradictory, say create a stone an omnipotent being can't lift, there is no
> reason to balk at His being able to do the further self-contradictory task: *to lift
> a stone He can't lift*. Well, I suppose I agree. If one swallows one impossibil-
> ity, then why not two? But the point, I suppose, of the atheistic argument is

that it poses a challenge to the rationality of belief in God. If one is prepared to dispense with rationality to preserve the belief, why not just reject the argument for no reason? Or, perhaps just as good, accept it and believe in God's omnipotence anyway.

Notwithstanding these eristical remarks, the Cartesian solution to the paradox is neither naïve nor irrational.

Moreover, the Cartesian may well point out that the Thomistic reply to the stone paradox was never really an option anyway. This is because, even though the paradox is often presented as a reductio with an embedded instance of disjunction elimination, the disjunctive sub-argument is entirely eliminable, as is premise (2). (This makes analetheic replies to the paradox nonstarters too, since they attack this premise of the canonical version of the paradox – cf. also Tedder & Badia 2018.) An equally good informal presentation of the paradox runs (cf. Drange 2003: 23):

1.* God is necessarily omnipotent.
2.* Therefore, God can create a stone which he cannot lift. [From (1*)]
3.* Therefore, it is possible that there is something that God cannot do. [From (2*)]
4.* But this is absurd. [From (1*) & (3*); QED]

This version of the argument is valid and more straightforward than the traditional presentation of the paradox. It deduces the first horn immediately from (1*) without needing to appeal to LEM at all. Consequently, there is no second horn to deny. Put formally, this version of the paradox runs:

Proof 2 Non-disjunctive form

i.*	$\Box \forall \varphi \Diamond A(\Theta, \varphi)$, w	A; Omnipotence
ii.*	R(w, w)	i*; MR
iii.*	$\forall \varphi \Diamond A(\Theta, \varphi)$, w	i*; MR
iv.*	$\Diamond A(\Theta, (\sim\Diamond A(\Theta, p)))$, w	iii*; $\forall$Eφ
v.*	R(w, w*)	iv*; $\Diamond$E
vi.*	$A(\Theta, (\sim\Diamond A(\Theta, p)))$, w*	iv*; $\Diamond$E
vii.*	$\sim\Diamond A(\Theta, p)$, w*	vi*; AE
viii.*	$\forall \varphi \Diamond A(\Theta, \varphi)$, w*	i*, v*; $\Box$E
ix.*	$\exists \varphi \sim \Diamond A(\Theta, \varphi)$, w*	vii*; $\exists$Iφ
x.*	$\sim\exists \varphi \sim \Diamond A(\Theta, \varphi)$, w*	viii*; Equiv.
xi.*	$\exists \varphi \sim \Diamond A(\Theta, \varphi) \wedge \sim\exists \varphi \sim \Diamond A(\Theta, \varphi)$, w*	ix*, x*; $\wedge$I
xii.*	$\bot$	xi*; LNC

The underlying logic of this version of the paradox is exactly as it was in the last formal presentation, except for line (iv*), which appeals to ∀Eφ.

I set out to complete three tasks in this section. The first is exegetical. Some deny that Descartes held that God could violate the laws of logic. And so I'll briefly digress to show that Descartes really did think God could do absolutely anything. The second is expository. I'll show how the Cartesian solution works to revise classical logic without rejecting it. And the third is argumentative. I'll offer arguments to motivate the Cartesian solution, and then I'll defend it from potential critiques and counterarguments. It is my contention that the Cartesian reply to the stone paradox is more plausible than the Thomistic one, despite the fact that it may not seem so at first glance.

Polypossibilist Modality

Descartes's views on divine omnipotence unfold over the course of a few scattered remarks in his Replies to Objections to his *Meditations* (Reply 5, to Gassendi; Reply 6, to Mersenne et al.); in his *Principles*; and then almost entirely throughout a series of letters to colleagues in the span of nearly twenty years (cf. La Croix 1984: 456–457). A few select passages should explain why some (e.g., Frankfurt 1964, 1977) have thought that Descartes believed that God could do literally anything.

Earlier, we reviewed St. Thomas's enthymemic argument for why God, although omnipotent, cannot do the logically impossible, which ran: Since logical contradictions are inconceivable, no omnipotent being can actualize a logical contradiction. In a sense, Descartes agrees with Aquinas's premise, but he nonetheless disagrees with Aquinas's inference. While logical contradictions may be inconceivable *to us*, they are not necessarily inconceivable *to God*:

> For my part, I know that my intellect is finite and God's power is infinite, and so I set no bounds to it. . . . And so I boldly assert that God can do everything which I conceive to be possible, but I am not so bold as to deny that He can do whatever conflicts with my understanding – I merely say that it involves a contradiction. . . . [For] I know that God can do more things than I can compass within my thoughts. [5 Feb. 1649]

(For a similar passage, see Descartes [25 April 1630].) More strongly, Descartes seems to suggest that for any given necessary truth, God could nonetheless falsify it if he wills:

> [W]e take refuge in the power of God, which we know to be infinite. . . . I do not think that we should ever say of anything that it cannot be brought about by God. For since everything involved in truth and goodness depends on His

omnipotence, I would not dare to say that God cannot make a mountain without a valley, or that one and two should not be three. . . . I merely say that He has given me such a mind that I cannot conceive a mountain without a valley, or an aggregate of one and two which is not three, and that such things involve a contradiction in my conception. [29 July 1648]

Additionally, Descartes believed that it is impossible that there exist vacuums in space; still, "God could remove a body from a container without [replacing it with] another body" [5 Feb. 1649].

Some scholars worry that Frankfurt's interpretation of Descartes would commit him to the position that Plantinga (1980: 92ff) calls *universal possibilism*, according to which, for every proposition, φ, φ is possibly the case. Frankfurt (1977: 42) seems to accept this consequence and writes that Descartes therefore thought that the "eternal truths are inherently as contingent as any other propositions." But critics demur, saying this interpretation faces two problems. First, it would seem to be inconsistent with other things Descartes says, as will be shown momentarily. And second, and more problematically, universal possibilism is logically absurd. Arguments are not usually offered to support this point, so I'll offer one now, which shows both that (i/i*) entails universal possibilism and also that universal possibilism entails a contradiction. The proof requires the same logic as before, except for the addition of $\Diamond$I:

- possibility introduction ($\Diamond$I) $(\exists w^*(R(w, w^*) \wedge (<p, w^*>)) \vdash <\Diamond p, w>)$

(Both $\Diamond$E and $\Diamond$I follow directly from K.) The argument runs:

Proof 3 Universal possibilist form

i.**	$\Box\forall\varphi\Diamond A(\Theta, \varphi), w$	A; Omnipotence
ii.**	$R(w, w)$	i**; MR
iii.**	$\forall\varphi\Diamond A(\Theta, \varphi), w$	i**; MR
iv.**	$\Diamond A(\Theta, p), w$	iii**; $\forall$Eφ
v.**	$R(w, w^*)$	iv**; $\Diamond$E
vi.**	$A(\Theta, p), w^*$	iv**; $\Diamond$E
vii.**	p, w^*	vi**; AE
viii.**	$\Diamond p, w$	v**, vii**; $\Diamond$I
ix.**	$\forall\varphi(\Diamond\varphi), w$	viii**; $\forall$Iφ
x.**	$\Diamond\sim\forall\varphi\Diamond A(\Theta, \varphi), w$	ix**; $\forall$Eφ
xi.**	$\sim\Diamond\sim\forall\varphi\Diamond A(\Theta, \varphi), w$	i**; Equiv.
xii.**	$\Diamond\sim\forall\varphi\Diamond A(\Theta, \varphi) \wedge \sim\Diamond\sim\forall\varphi\Diamond A(\Theta, \varphi), w$	x**, xi**; $\wedge$I
xiii.**	$\bot$	xii**; LNC

Proof 3 may be understood as yet a third formal version of the stone paradox.

Against Frankfurt, Curley (1984) instead proposes that Descartes was committed only to *limited possibilism*, according to which, for every proposition, φ, possibly φ is possibly the case ($\forall\varphi(\diamond\diamond\varphi)$), which does not entail that every proposition is possibly the case, simplicter ($\forall\varphi(\diamond\diamond\varphi) \not\vdash \forall\varphi(\diamond\varphi)$). The limited possibilist interpretation would support Descartes's claims that there are indeed necessary truths, since it is prima facie consistent to suppose that some truth is necessary and at the same time possibly-possibly false (i.e., not necessarily necessary). In support of this interpretation, Curley (1984: 573) cites Descartes's summary in *Le Monde*, where Descartes (1677/1996) writes: "I showed what were the laws of nature, and without basing my arguments on any other principle than the infinite perfections of God, I tried to show that, even if God had created several worlds, there could not be any in which they would fail to be observed." This passage suggests that he did think the laws of nature are in some sense necessarily true, that is, not possibly false.

Either possibilist interpretation would commit Descartes to a very unusual modal metaphysics and an even more unusual modal logic, such as C. I. Lewis's S6, S7, or S8 modal systems (cf. Curley 1984: sect. 6). (The limited possibilist interpretation would also commit Descartes to the denial of *modal transitivity*, which is standard in most contemporary analytic metaphysicians' preferred modal logic, S5 – cf. Sider 2010: ch. 6; Bassford 2019.) Geach (1973: 11) famously complains about both interpretations:

> In recent years, unsound philosophies have been defended by what I may call *shyster logicians*: some of the more dubious recent developments of modal logic could certainly be used to defend Descartes. A system in which "possibly p" was a theorem – in which everything is possible – has indeed never been taken seriously; but modal logicians have taken seriously systems in which "possibly possibly p", or again "it is not necessary that necessarily p", would be a theorem for arbitrary interpretation of "p". What is more, some modern modal logicians notoriously take possible worlds very seriously ... People who take *both* things seriously ... would say: You mention any impossibility, and there's a possible world in which that isn't impossible but possible. And this is even further away out than Descartes would wish to go; for he would certainly not wish to say that "It is possible that God should not exist" is even *possibly* true. So *a fortiori* a shyster logician could fadge up a case for Descartes.

La Croix (1984: 456ff) instead proposes that Descartes was only committed to a position which I'll call *counterpossibilism*. This is the position according to which God merely *could have* made it the case that laws of logic and metaphysics are false, but not that he currently can or even possibly can.

This is a counterfactual interpretation of God's ability to violate the laws of nature (cf. Lewis 1973/2005, 1979). The following passage supports this interpretation:

> I turn to the difficulty of conceiving how it was free and indifferent for God to make it not be true that the three angles of a triangle were equal to two right angles, or in general that contradictories could not be true together. It is easy to dispel this difficulty by considering that the power of God cannot have any limits, and that our mind is finite and so created as to be able to conceive as possible things which God has wished to be in fact possible, but not to be able to conceive as possible things which God *could have made possible*, but which he has *in fact wished to make impossible*. [2 May 1644]

Given Descartes's claim that the laws of nature are necessary, this would entail that all claims about what God *could have* done are vacuously true, since, having created the laws as they are, it is necessarily false that God creates them differently (cf. Starr 2021). But the counterpossibilist interpretation cannot be sustained. As noted earlier, God's omnitemporality is best understood as eternality, not sempiternity. On this point, Descartes seems to agree with St. Peter: "You ask what God did in order to produce [the eternal truths]. I reply that *from all eternity* he willed and understood them to be, and by that very fact he created them" [27 May 1630] (cf. also 1647/1996: pt. 1, sects. 14, 22–23). But for an eternal being like God, what God could have done and what God can do are one and the same.

Kaufman (2002: 33ff) instead proposes that Descartes was a Thomist about God's omnipotence after all. Indeed, even here, there are passages that may support this interpretation. For example, in writing of the possibility that God could change the past, Descartes writes: "[W]e do not ... perceive it to be possible for what is done to be undone – on the contrary, we perceive it to be altogether impossible, and so it is no defect of power in God not to do it" [5 Feb. 1649]. But, more likely, this is simply an instance of inconsistency in Descartes's letters, rather than a reasonable interpretation of Descartes's considered views on omnipotence, given all of the other passages we've examined so far. Alternatively, Descartes may have intentionally presented his views differently depending on with whom he was conversing, which would also explain the inconsistency.

Finally, McFetridge (1990), Conee (1991: 449, 454ff), and Tedder (2020) propose that Descartes was merely committed to a form of what I'll call *polypossibilism*. This is the position according to which there are many different kinds of modality. So, strictly speaking, a claim of the form "possibly p" is semantically ambiguous. Indeed, many contemporary analytic metaethicists distinguish between what is *practically possible* vs. what is *feasible* vs. what is *boulomaically possible* (i.e., possible given one's desires/goals) (cf. Bassford 2022: sect. 2; Swanson 2008). Contemporary epistemologists likewise distinguish between what is *epistemically possible* vs. *alethically possible*. And contemporary analytic metaphysicians similarly distinguish between various forms of nomic possibility, such as what is *physically possible* vs. *metaphysically possible* vs. *logically possible*, as we have been speaking here (cf. Mallozzi, Vaidya, & Wallner 2021; Bassford & Dolson *forthcoming*). Descartes seems to have recognized a distinction between what is *theologically possible* (possible by the power of God) vs. *nontheologically* possible (possible otherwise). Descartes:

> We . . . know that it is impossible that there should exist atoms, that is, pieces of matter that are by their very nature indivisible. . . . [Nonetheless] [e]ven if we imagine that God has chosen to bring it about that some particle of matter is incapable of being divided into smaller particles, it will still not be correct, strictly speaking, to call this particle indivisible. For, by making it indivisible by any of his creatures, God could certainly not thereby take away his own power of dividing it, since it is quite impossible for him to diminish his own power. (1647/1996: pt. 2, sect. 20)

We can accordingly distinguish between two sets of modal operators in the present discussion. Following Tedder, let "◇" and "□" designate nontheological modality, and let "◆" and "■" designate theological modality. In saying that God can do anything, this interpretation would have it that Descartes means to express only:

$$<\forall\varphi\blacklozenge A(\Theta, \varphi), w >$$

The polypossibilist interpretation of Descartes appears superior to its competitors, in that it can make sense of all the previous passages, whereas the rest cannot say the same. Notably, this interpretation allows Descartes to say that the laws of nature are indeed (nontheologically) necessary, but not (theologically) necessary. These claims are consistent, since a single proposition can be necessary according to one type of modality (e.g., metaphysical necessity) without at the same time being necessary according to another (e.g., logical necessity). Therefore, while Descartes *may* have accepted universal possibilism with respect to theological modality, he seems to have denied it with respect to nontheological modality. (But more on this later.)

Some interpretations of Descartes are consistent with a Cartesian solution to the stone paradox, and some are not. The limited possibilist about God's power cannot take the Cartesian line, since we are asking whether God *could* create such a stone, not whether he *possibly could* create such a stone. Similarly for the counterpossibilist interpretation, since, again, we are asking what God *could* do, not simply what he *could have* done. The universal possibilist can take the

Cartesian line, as Frankfurt (1969) in fact has done. But so too can the poly-possibilist, since both the universal possibilist and the polypossibilist hold that God can indeed do anything. Since the polypossibilist interpretation of Descartes would seem to be the most charitable account of Descartes, I conclude that Descartes would evidently endorse a Cartesian solution to the stone paradox.

Sub Precepto Divino

Let's put aside exegesis and return to the primary dialectic. Cartesians hold that God can do all things, even the logically impossible – such as creating and then lifting an unliftable stone. Why might one think this? Two arguments suggest themselves. The first is indirect; the second, direct. The first argument runs: Suppose that God cannot act contrary to the laws of logic. If so, then the analytic theist must deny God's *aseity*, which is inconsistent with classical theism. Divine aseity implies that neither God nor his activities are dependent on anything else in any way (cf. Brower 2011; Adams & Robson 2020). But if God cannot violate the laws of logic, then this would mean that his activities are dependent on something external to him – viz., laws of logic. For this reason, we should conclude that God could freely change or otherwise violate the laws of logic. Descartes:

> The mathematical truths which you call eternal have been laid down by God and depend on Him entirely no less than the rest of his creatures. Indeed to say that these truths are independent of God is to talk of Him as if He were Jupiter or Saturn and to subject Him to the Styx and Fates. Please do not hesitate to assert and proclaim everywhere that it is God who has laid down these laws in nature just as a king lays down laws in his kingdom. . . . It will be said that if God has established these truths He could change them as a king changes his laws. To this the answer is: "Yes he can, if his will can change." [15 April 1630] (For a similar passage, see Descartes 1642/1970: reply 6, sect. 8.)

The second argument is direct. First premise: God is the creator and sustainer of everything that exists (*extra Deum*). Or, as Descartes puts it: "There is no doubt that if God withdrew his cooperation, everything which he has created would go to nothing; because all things were nothing until God created them and provided his cooperation" [Aug. 1641]. Second premise: God is perfectly free. Third premise: An agent is free with respect to some action only if they could choose to do it and they could choose to refrain from doing it (cf. Frankfurt 1969; Alanen 1985: sect. 5). From the first premise, we can infer that God created and sustains even the laws of logic. From the second premise, we can infer that his creation and maintenance of these laws have been done freely. And from the third, we can infer that he could have chosen not to create the laws as they are (perhaps by creating different laws, or by creating no laws at all) and that he can choose to cease sustaining the laws as they are (perhaps by replacing them with different laws, or by annihilating them altogether). But if God can change or otherwise annihilate the laws of logic, then so too can he choose to act contrary to them, if he wills. Descartes:

> You ask me by what kind of causality God established the eternal truths. I reply: by the same kind of causality as he created all things, that is to say, as the efficient and total cause. For it is certain that he is no less the author of creatures' essence than he is of their existence; and this essence is nothing other than the eternal truths. . . . I know that God is the author of everything and that these truths are something and consequently that he is their author. . . . You ask also what necessitated God to create these truths; and I reply that just as He was free not to create the world, so He was no less free to make it untrue that all the lines drawn from the center of a circle to its circumference are equal. And it is certain that these truths are no more necessarily attached to his essence than other creatures are. [27 May 1630] (For similar passages, see Descartes 1642/1970: reply 6, sects. 6, 8.)

A critic might object to the Cartesian arguments in one of three ways. First, Descartes writes that God could change the laws of logic on the condition that "his will can change." But, a critic may say, God is essentially *immutable*, and so his will cannot change. Consequently, we should not conclude that God can actually violate the laws of logic, but only that, per impossibile, were his will to change, he could. But even the Thomist can accept this conditional; Aquinas (1274/1952: ST, pt. 1, Q25, A3): "For there is no reason why a conditional proposition should not be true, though both the antecedent and consequent are impossible: as if one were to say: 'If man is a donkey, he has four feet.'" In reply, I'll say that we need not follow Descartes's conditional conclusion on this point. As Malebranche (1678/1997: eluc. 10) rightly notes, just because God's will is immutable, this does not mean that the product of his will must be immutable, too. Otherwise divine immutability would imply *necessitarianism*, that everything is necessary. This does not seem to be the case (but see, e.g., Spinoza 1677/2005; Koistinen 2003; Rowe 2002). So, God's will might remain the same, even if the laws of logic might nonetheless change, and this would simply be another mutable product of his immutable will.

Second, a critic might say that the classical theist need not accept that God created and sustains the laws of logic. Consider logical tautologies, for example, "$(p \equiv p)$." Propositions like these are arguably true not because of God but simply as a matter of logical syntax (cf. Scotus c. 1300/1987: *Ordinatio*, pt. 1, dist. 43; Lemmon 1965/1969: 69; Fine 2010). Moreover, many logical tautologies have nothing to do with existence; for example, "A unicorn is a unicorn" is true, even though no unicorns exist. But a creator and sustainer must only be posited for things that exist, not for things that do not exist, too (cf. Suárez 1597/1983: disp. 31, sect. 12). In reply, I'll say that, in stating the doctrine of divine aseity earlier, I stated only a necessary condition of it. Divine aseity holds that not only is God independent of everything else, but also that everything else is dependent on him. In this way, God is said to be both ontologically and explanatorily prior to everything else (cf. Laughlin 2009; Baddorf 2017). Now, syntax is ultimately a creation of God, too. And so, even if syntax explains a tautology's truth, we might then ask: What explains *this* fact? The classical theist says that all explanations ought ultimately to bottom out with God. Descartes:

> As for the eternal truths, I say once more that they are true or possible only because God knows them as true or possible. They are not known as true by God in any way which would imply that they are true independently of Him. If men really understood the sense of their words they could never say without blasphemy that the truth of anything is prior to the knowledge which God has of it. ... So we must not say that if God did not exist nonetheless these truths would be true; for the existence of God is the first and most eternal of all possible truths and the one from which alone all others derive.

So, while a logical truth's syntax may be the *proximate* grounds for its being true, syntax alone cannot be a tautology's *ultimate* grounds.

Finally, a critic may concede to Descartes that God is the creator and sustainer of the laws of logic (cf. Aquinas 1274/1952: ST, pt. 1 of 2, Q16, A7). But they may deny that they must be grounded in God's *will*, as Descartes suggests. The position according to which it is God's will that grounds the laws of reality is called *divine voluntarism* (sometimes also *divine positivism*), which was likewise held by Ockham and Henry of Ghent (cf. Bittle 1939: ch. 7; Alanen 1985: sect. 7; Porro 2014: sect. 7). Aquinas (1274/1952: ST, pt. 1, Q16, A7) and Pseudo-Grosseteste (c. 1277/1957), on the other hand, contend that the eternal truths are instead grounded in God's *intellect* (cf. Alanen 1985: sect. 1). The position according to which it is God's intellect that grounds the laws of reality is called *divine rationalism* (cf. Clark 1971; Alanen 1988: 190–191). However, whereas it makes sense to speak of God's will being perfectly free, it does not make sense to speak of his intellect as free. Consequently, if it is God's intellect that grounds the eternal truths, then it would not follow that God could act contrary to them, since that would be irrational and therefore inconsistent with God's omniscience.

A Cartesian might offer three replies to this final objection. Suárez (1597/1983: DM, bk. 31, sect. 12) complains that the divine intellect cannot be the grounds of eternal truths because the intellectual faculty is entirely *speculative*, not *active*. By this Suárez means that, in general, something is known because it is true; it is not true because it is known; and so divine rationalism would seem to unacceptably reverse the order of explanation between knowledge and truth. This reply, however, is not very plausible, because Thomists have traditionally held that even though, for creatures, knowledge is an effect, for God, it is instead a cause (cf. Bassford 2021: sect. 6). Alternatively, Descartes [6 May 1630] replies that to accept divine rationalism would entail denying divine incomprehensibility. We understand well many necessary truths; and so if these necessary truths exist necessarily in God's intellect, then we must also partially understand his intellect. But this is absurd, not to say "heretical" (but see Mavrodes 1988 on this point; cf. also Bassford 2020). Finally, the Cartesian might appeal to divine simplicity to remind the critic that, as perfectly simple, there is no real distinction between God's will and God's intellect. Descartes: "[I]f we would know the immensity of his power we should not . . . conceive any precedence or priority between his understanding and his will; for the idea which we have of God teaches us that there is in him only a single activity, entirely simple and entirely pure" [2 May 1644]. So, if the critic would prefer, we can say that it is simply God's *free essence* that grounds the laws of logic; in which case, he might still act contrary to them (cf. Bittle 1939: ch. 7; Alanen 1988: 191).

Power Beyond Possibility

Polypossibilist Cartesianism about divine omnipotence holds that the laws of logic are nontheologically necessary but theologically contingent, because God could change, annihilate, or otherwise violate them, if he wills. I said that this position is prima facie coherent, since it is possible for a proposition to be necessary according to one type of modality without being necessary according to another type. Now I need to say much more about this proposal. First, it is not *always* coherent to say that a proposition is necessary in one sense but not in another; it is incoherent, for example, to say that whereas p may be metaphysically necessary, it is nonetheless physically contingent, since whatever is physically contingent must also be metaphysically contingent. And so I need to explain how exactly theological modality relates to nontheological modality such that polypossibilist Cartesianism is demonstrated to be coherent. Second, I have suggested that the Cartesian should say only that God's omnipotence amounts to this: $<\forall\varphi\blacklozenge A(\Theta, \varphi), w>$. But classical theists hold that God's omnipotence is essential (i.e., *necessary*) to him. So, I need to specify how the necessity operator should be understood in the classical theist's claim that God is necessarily omnipotent.

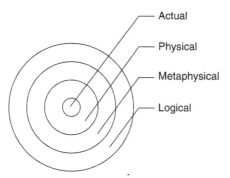

— Actual

— Physical

— Metaphysical

— Logical

Figure 3 Modal grades of logical space

How does theological modality relate to nontheological modality? I propose that the Cartesian answer this question by appealing to the notion of *modal grade*. Contemporary analytic metaphysics not only recognize different types of alethic modality, but they also propose that each modality is of different modal strength. From the perspective of *possibility*, logical possibility is understood to be the weakest modal grade. A proposition is logically possible (relative to the actual world) just in case it is consistent with the laws of logic (e.g., LNC, LEM, and so on). Metaphysical possibility is stronger than logical possibility. A proposition is metaphysically possible (relative to the actual world) just in case it is consistent with both our logical and metaphysical laws (e.g., ENN, LSC, and so on). Finally, physical possibility is the strongest of the three. A proposition is physically possible (relative to the actual world) just in case it is consistent with our laws of logic, our metaphysical laws, and our physical laws. In this way, all of the possible worlds in logical space form a kind of "onion" structure of nested spheres around the actual world (Figure 3): The actual world is a subset of the physically possible worlds, which are a subset of the metaphysically possible worlds, which are a subset of the logically possible worlds (cf. Lewis 1973/2005: Bassford & Dolson *forthcoming*).

From the perspective of *necessity*, logical necessity is thought to be the strongest modal grade, since absolutely every world in logical space is thought to be consistent with the laws of logic; and metaphysical and physical necessity are weaker, since only a subset of the logically possible worlds shares our metaphysical laws, and only a subset of the metaphysically possible worlds shares our physical laws. Consequently, it is possible, for instance, for a proposition to be logically contingent while nonetheless being metaphysically necessary, but it is not possible, for instance, for a proposition to be physically contingent while being metaphysically necessary. To further disambiguate our "◇" and "□" modal operators, we can add subscripts to each, designating the

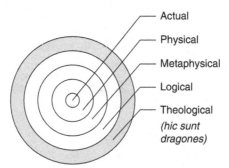

Figure 4 Modal grades of theological space

type of possibility or necessity under consideration: "$\diamond_L$" and "$\square_L$," for logical modality; "$\diamond_M$" and "$\square_M$," for metaphysical modality; and "$\diamond_P$" and "$\square_P$," for physical modality.

I propose that the analytic theist add another modal grade into their model of logical space. Since we have proposed that a proposition may be logically necessary without being theologically necessary, we should therefore add a grade to the outer ring of our modal onion (Figure 4).

So, we can say that theological possibility is the weakest form of modality, and theological necessity is therefore the strongest. Another way to put this is that, whereas every other modal operator comes packaged with various *inheritance rules*, such that, for example, "$<\diamond_L(p), w>$" entails that there is a world, w*, accessible from w, $<p, w^*>$, and w* inherits all of the logical laws of w; a proposition of the form "$<\blacklozenge(p), w>$" does not require that an accessible world inherit any laws from w at all, not even w's logical laws. By expanding logical space in this way, the Cartesian can therefore demonstrate that their polypossibilist proposal is consistent. So, even though it is physically necessary that no object travel faster than the speed of light, it is nonetheless theologically possible for God to create a superluminal object; even though it is metaphysically necessary that nothing come from nothing, it is nonetheless theologically possible for God to create something ex nihilo; and even though it is logically necessary that no one squares a circle or climbs an actually infinite staircase or correctly calculates that 2 + 2 = 5, it is nonetheless theologically possible for God to do all of these things and more.

Nonnormal Impossible Worlds

In adding a grade of modality *beyond* the limits of logical necessity, my proposal has thereby also added *impossible worlds* into logical space. The notion of an impossible world is a familiar one in contemporary analytic philosophy, admitting of many applications (cf. Nolan 2021; Berto & Jago 2018: sect. 2). In fact, anyone who accepts modal grades is already committed to impossible worlds in some sense, since, as we said, a proposition may be, for example, metaphysically possible but not physically possible; hence, from the perspective of physical modality, a world at which such a proposition obtains would be a physically impossible world. My proposal specifically introduces *logically impossible worlds* into the modal domain.

Logically impossible worlds are generally characterized in one of two ways (cf. Tanaka 2018; Sandgren & Tanaka 2020). Sometimes impossible worlds are characterized as worlds in which the laws of logic fail, which is consistent with the world having *no* laws of logic at all. Alternatively, impossible worlds are sometimes characterized as worlds having *nonclassical* logical laws. In both interpretations, a contradiction may obtain, though a contradiction need not actually obtain. The first sort of worlds are *anarchic*, whereas the second are merely *nonnormal* (cf. Kripke 1965; Priest 1992, 2008a: 171–175). In proposing that the Cartesian appeal to logically impossible worlds, I suggest that the Cartesian introduce nonnormal impossible worlds into the modal domain. There are many varieties of nonclassical logic that permit contradictions to obtain. The Cusanists have explored several suitable ones for making sense of divine omnipotence. Recall that the Cusanist says that a nonclassical logic regulates the actual world (and God's actual activity at it); by contrast, the Cartesian need say only that such logics regulate some impossible worlds (and God's possible activity at them). Even so, the Cartesian can borrow the Cusanists' preferred logics in understanding merely theologically possible worlds (cf. Beall & Cotnoir 2017; Beall 2017, 2019, 2021; Cotnoir 2017, 2019).

Two nonclassical logics seem eminently suitable for modeling the logic of worlds where God actualizes a contradiction. The first is the Logic of Paradox, LP (cf. Priest 1979, 1987); and the second is RM_3 (cf. Anderson & Bellnap 1975) (cf. also Priest 2008a: ch. 7; Beall & van Fraassen 2003: ch. 8). Both are polyvalent logics, in that they both propose that a proposition may have one of *three* truth-values: 1, 0, or ½. How to interpret this third value is a matter of controversy; dialetheists interpret it as a *glut*, both true and false; analetheists interpret it as a *gap*, neither true nor false (cf. Beall & Ripley 2004). I follow the dialetheists here. LP and RM_3 encode similar semantics, borrowing from the logic Strong Kleene, K_3 (cf. Kleene 1952: sect. 64). They both agree with K_3 with respect to "~," "∧," and "∨": Negation flips the proposition's polarity, from 1 to 0, 0 to 1, or ½ to ½; a conjunction takes the lower-bound value of its conjuncts; and a disjunction takes the upper-bound value of its disjuncts. The classical logic (CL) truth tables:

$\sim_{CL}$	
1	0
0	1

$\wedge_{CL}$	1	0
1	1	0
0	0	0

$\vee_{CL}$	1	0
1	1	1
0	1	0

$\supset_{CL}$	1	0
1	1	0
0	1	1

The K_3 truth tables:

$\sim_{K3}$	
1	0
½	½
0	1

$\wedge_{K3}$	1	½	0
1	1	½	0
½	½	½	0
0	0	0	0

$\vee_{K3}$	1	½	0
1	1	1	1
½	1	½	½
0	1	½	0

LP and RM$_3$ disagree with one another with respect to "$\supset$." LP follows K$_3$ (and CL) in defining it in terms of "$\sim$" and "$\vee$" (($p \supset q) \equiv (\sim p \vee q)$). RM$_3$ instead offers a new semantic for the material conditional (or offers a new conditional that uses the same symbol). This is not immediately pertinent to the present discussion, but it should be noted anyway:

$\supset_{K3/LP}$	1	½	0
1	1	½	0
½	1	½	½
0	1	1	1

$\supset_{RM3}$	1	½	0
1	1	0	0
½	1	½	0
0	1	1	1

LP and RM$_3$, however, both disagree with K$_3$ with respect to their *designated values*. K$_3$ follows CL in taking only 1 as designated. *Validity* is defined in terms of designated values: An inference is valid just in case there is no truth-functional interpretation that assigns all the premises a designated value, but assigns the conclusion an undesignated one. Consequently, in K$_3$, no valid inference concludes with a proposition having the value ½. In this way, gluts are in some sense *unassertable* in K$_3$, even though they are semantically recognized. In LP and RM$_3$, on the other hand, both 1 and ½ are designated. Consequently, in both systems, one can validly reason *from* and *to* propositions taking the value ½. Certain valid inferential patterns in CL are invalid in LP and RM$_3$. For example, MP is invalid in LP (($p \supset q$), $p \nvdash_{LP} q$). To see why this is so, suppose $v(p) = $ ½ and $v(q) = 0$; then $v(p \supset q) = $ ½; but then both premises have designated values, but the conclusion does not. MP is valid in RM$_3$, but then other common inferences are not – for example, ($q \nvdash_{RM3} (p \supset q)$). Most notably, in both systems, LNC fails. After all, if $v(p) = $ ½, then $v(\sim p) = $ ½, from which it follows that v $(p \wedge \sim p) = $ ½ too; which is designated. And ECQ fails too (($p \wedge \sim p) \nvdash q$). Just let $v(p \wedge \sim p) = $ ½ and $v(q) = 0$; then the premise is designated but the conclusion is not. These are therefore paraconsistent logics.

Now let's connect our theological modals with our LP/RM_3 nonnormal impossible worlds. I propose that: $v(<\blacklozenge p, w>) = 1$ only if there is some world, w^*, such that $R(w, w^*)$, w^* need not inherit any laws from w (but in which case is nonetheless regulated by either LP or RM_3 nonclassical logic), and $v(<p, w^*>) = 1$ or ½. And: $v(<\blacksquare p, w>) = 1$ only if every world, w^*, is such that $R(w, w^*)$, w^* need not inherit any laws from w (but in which case is nonetheless regulated by either LP or RM_3), and $v(<p, w^*>) = 1$ or ½. (For proposals on how quantifiers might work within this system, see Priest 2008a: ch. 21; Beall & Cotnoir 2017.)

Necessary Omnipotence

How should the Cartesian interpret the necessity operator in the classical theist's claim that God is "necessarily" omnipotent? The Cartesian has two options here. The Cartesian might understand the "□" in terms of theological necessity or in terms of nontheological necessity. If they take the first tack, then they should say that God's necessary omnipotence amounts to the claim that:

$$<\blacksquare\forall\varphi\blacklozenge A(\Theta, \varphi), w >$$

And if they take the second tack, then they should say that God's necessary omnipotence amounts to the claim that it is metaphysically necessary that he is omnipotent:

$$<\Box_M\forall\varphi\blacklozenge A(\Theta, \varphi), w >$$

Each interpretation would work differently within a reply to the stone paradox. Consider Proof 1 and Proof 2. A proponent of the theological interpretation can object that world w^* is introduced in both paradoxes to discharge a claim about theological possibility. But a merely theologically possible world need not inherit any of the logical laws of the actual world. And so, we cannot assume that w^* is regulated by our laws of logic, such as the LNC. Consequently, they will advise that the Cartesian reject lines (xi) and (xii*). A proponent of the metaphysical interpretation, on the other hand, should object to the paradox sooner in both proofs. Again, world w^* is introduced in both proofs to discharge a claim about theological possibility. But then the paradox discharges a claim about metaphysical necessity into w^*. But to do so is to assume that w^* is regulated by the same metaphysical laws as w, which is unwarranted, since what is metaphysically necessary need not also be theologically necessary. Consequently, they will instead advise the Cartesian to reject lines (viii) and (viii*).

I propose the Cartesian follow the metaphysical interpretation of God's necessary omnipotence. Three arguments support this interpretation over the theological one. The first is that the claim "God is necessarily omnipotent" is intuitively a truth of neither physics nor logic, but it may plausibly be understood as a metaphysical truth. The second is that analytic theists usually say that God is *necessarily* omnipotent only because they say that God is *essentially* omnipotent. But claims about the essence of a thing entail only metaphysically necessary truths about it. And the third is that if one accepts the theological interpretation of God's necessary omnipotence, then they risk running headlong into the same paradox that faces Frankfurt's interpretation of Descartes. In Proof 3, we saw that a commitment to universal possibilism would entail a contradiction in the actual world. Supposing that the merely theologically possible worlds are governed by K, the same argument can be used here – swapping out "◇" for "◆" and "□" for "■" – to demonstrate that the theological interpretation of the necessity operator would likewise lead to both universal possibilism and a contradiction in the actual world. Therefore, this interpretation may be consistent with Cusanism, but it is not consistent with Cartesianism, according to which there are no actually true contradictions, but only possibly true ones. By contrast, the metaphysical interpretation can escape this objection. A Cartesian who accepts the metaphysical interpretation would simply deny that the two modals in (xii**) are identical; in which case no contradiction follows.

So, on my preferred interpretation, the analytic theist should say:

$$\Box_M \forall \varphi \blacklozenge A(\Theta, \varphi)$$

that is, that it is *metaphysically necessary* that it is *theologically possible* for God to actualize any proposition. This includes logical contradictions:

$$\blacklozenge A(\Theta, (p \land \sim p))$$

This reply can circumvent all three formal proofs of the stone paradox. Moreover, with the logical apparatus I've assigned it, it can also be shown to be logically coherent, according to established principles of mathematical logic and paraconsistency. Semantically, these claims just entail that there are some *logically impossible worlds* where God has actualized a contradiction. However, at those worlds, $v(p) = \frac{1}{2} = v(\sim p)$, which is acceptable in the LP/RM$_3$ logics governing our impossible worlds.

God-Talk: The Way of Paradox

Let's take stock. The Cartesian contends that God's omnipotence permits him to do anything, even the logically impossible. So far, I've been offering a sympathetic survey of Cartesian arguments for this unrestricted conception of omnipotence and explaining how the Cartesian solution to the stone paradox would work. The best arguments for thinking that God's power is absolutely unrestricted are two. First, God exists and acts *a se*; so, he and his activity are not dependent on the laws of logic. Second, God freely created and sustains the laws of logic; so, he could cease sustaining them and act contrary to them, if he wills. I said that the best way to make sense of the Cartesian solution to the stone paradox, then, is to introduce a new set of modal operators, corresponding to an even weaker grade of modality than logical possibility; and then to suppose that the impossible worlds answering to them may be nonnormal and regulated by LP or RM₃ nonclassical logic, at which contradictions may permissibly occur. This amounts to the claim that the laws of CL are *logically necessary*, but they are not theologically necessary: *God's potentiality is superlogical.* I turn now from argument to defense. I raise the question: Is the Cartesian account of God's omnipotence plausible? I answer that it is. I'll now rehearse two potential objections to the proposal and defend it from them. The first is theological, and the second is logical.

A critic might complain that Cartesianism is inconsistent with revealed classical theological traditions. A Christian complaint to this effect is most forthcoming. Following the Seven Councils, Christian theologians have insisted that all good bibliology, Christology, pneumatology, soteriology, and so on conform to principles of CL. Theology itself is so named so as to designate that it is *logical* speech about God, which is understood to mean, minimally, *noncontradictory* speech. Christian scripture would seem to lend support to this insistence: "In the beginning was the Logos, and the Logos was with God, and the Logos was God. ... Through [the Logos] all things were made; without [the Logos] nothing was made that has been made" (John 1:1–3). So, an orthodox classical theologian might say that to deny CL is nonconservative from the perspective of the Christian tradition, which is deeply committed to God not being thought or spoken about in contradictions. But since Cartesianism permits contradictory speech about God, it follows that it is too heterodoxic to accept.

I'll offer three replies to this critique. My first reply is just that many other religions have permitted contradictory speech in their revealed traditions and have thought, moreover, that such speech is invaluable for expressing the divine. This is especially true in certain Eastern religions, such as Daoism (cf. Hu 1922/1963: pt. 4, ch. 2), Buddhism (cf. Suzuki 1934: ch. 4; Tillemans 1999: ch. 9; Cotnoir 2015), and Hinduism (cf. Chaudhuri 1954). In Hinduism, for example, Brahman, the Great Soul of the World, is said to include every property of the world, active/passive, positive/negative, good/evil, and so on – and thus to completely transcend logic and human rational thought altogether. I am inclined to think that, whenever the Abrahamic theist can learn from other religions around the world, they ought to relish the opportunity, for they might even learn more about God. So, even if the critic is right that Cartesianism is doxologically out of step with certain revealed traditions, that is not decisive grounds for rejecting it.

My second reply is that, what's more, there is also a long Christian tradition of permitting contradictory speech in theology, which the critic has ignored. The Psalms teach us of "riddles," or "dark sayings" (Psalms 78:2–3); and in Christian scripture, St. Paul characterizes Christian life itself as a kind of enigma, writing: "We are afflicted in every way, but not crushed; perplexed, but not driven to despair; persecuted, but not forsaken; struck down, but not destroyed ... for while we live, we are always being given up to death for Jesus's sake" (2 Corinthians 4:8–10). Kierkegaard famously called the doctrine of the incarnation an "absolute paradox" and so Christian faith a "contradiction," which he was nonetheless willing to accept (cf. Evans 2008; cf. also Trakakis 1997: sect. 4). Moreover, medieval theologians debated denying certain logical principles when applied to God; for example, *expository syllogistic* reasoning was called into question when discussing the Trinity (cf. Buridan c. 1335: Q4; Lagerlund 2022; Uckelman 2009: ch. 7, appx. C; Trakakis 1997: sect. 3; Evans 1994: 60–66; Moody 1966/1975).

Daoists and Buddhists have been inclined to accept certain true dialetheia about the divine on the grounds that ultimate reality is ultimately indeterminate. But all speech is determinate. So, the way we can speak most truly of the ultimate reality is in terms of dialetheia (cf. Northrop 1947/1983: ch. 23). Neoplatonist dialetheic theists expressed a similar intuition to the Hindu's – that the divine is ultimately overdeterminate, and that our language is too impoverished to express ultimate reality besides by contradictions (cf. Nicholas of Cusa 1440/1969: chs. 2–3; cf. also Plotinus c. 253/1952: *Ennead*, bk. 5, ch. 4; Knepper 2008). The classical theist does not share these intuitions, but they do express the intuition that ultimate reality (viz., God) is ultimately transcendent and fundamentally unlike any creature: "To whom then will you liken God, or what likeness compare with him?" (Isaiah 40:18). For this reason, there is a rich tradition in Abrahamic theology pertaining to how exactly we can speak truly of God (cf. Evans 1994: 55–60). The problem is that all human language seems to have developed to engage with and describe nontranscendent reality; and so all human language would seem to be inadequate to describe God (cf. Macquarrie 1967: chs. 1–3).

In response to this problem, classical Christian theologians have proposed a number of putative solutions. Since literal, affirmative speech would seem to be entirely inappropriate to describe God, some have contended that we should simply *remain silent* about the subject. Wittgenstein (1922/2003: sect. 7): "Whereof one cannot speak, thereof one must be silent." This is the Way of Silence. Others have contended that theologians should instead speak of God only in *negative propositions*. Clement of Alexandria (c. 200: bk. 5, ch. 11): "[A]bstracting all that belongs to bodies and things ... we may reach somehow to the conception of the Almighty, knowing not what He is, but what He is not." This is the Way of Negation. Others have contended that theologians should speak of God *analogically* (or, better, *metaphorically*) (cf. Cotnoir 2019: sect. 4.1; Bonevac 2012; cf. Anselm 1076/1975: chs. 14–16). This is the Way of Analogy.

Still others have contended that theologians should instead speak of God *paradoxically*, in well-chosen contradictions (cf. Barth 1936/1949: ch. 1, sect. 5; Rehnman 2008; Macquarrie 1967: ch. 10). This is the Way of Paradox. All four traditions are well documented in received Christian tradition and have many proponents, both classical and contemporary. Consequently, Cartesianism about God's omnipotence is not so radical as the critic suggests, since it merely recommends we follow the Way of Paradox when speaking of the extent of God's power. Macquarrie (1967: 30) asks: "Is it possible then that [theological] language can be stretched in such apparently illogical ways, so as to enable us to see something that language in its ordinary usages would miss? And if so, how is this possible? ... Are there perhaps other logics, or other modes of syntax, that have their legitimate uses?" I suggest that a theological modal logic of impossible worlds governed by LP or RM_3 nonclassical logic may fit this bill.

My final reply to the theological complaint is that there are several ways of interpreting the metaphysical significance of the Cartesian's proposed possible dialetheia (cf. Mares 2004: sect. 1). Some who accept true contradictions suppose that there are genuinely contradictory states of affairs in modal reality (in general, or with respect to God) (cf. Yagisawa 1988, 2010). This is *metaphysical dialetheism*. Other dialetheists are not committed to contradictory modal facts; rather, they say that dialetheia emerge as the result of our language (in general, or with respect to God) (cf. Beall & Cotnoir 2017; Beall 2011; Cotnoir 2017: sect. 7). This is *semantic dialetheism*. Still others propose that dialetheia neither correspond to modal facts nor are merely a product of our language; rather, dialetheia emerge as a result of our own epistemic limitations (in general, or with respect to God). This is *epistemic dialetheism*, which Descartes (1629–1649/1970) seems to have endorsed (cf. also Frankfurt 1977: sect. 6):

> [I]t is possible to know that God is infinite and all-powerful although our soul, being finite, cannot comprehend or conceive Him. In the same way we can touch a mountain with our hands but we cannot put our arms around it as we could put them around a tree or something else not too large for them. To comprehend something is to embrace it in one's thoughts; to know something it is sufficient to touch it with one's thought. [27 May 1630]

So, in saying, then, that God can lift even an unliftable stone, we can say with Descartes: "I say that I know this, not that I can conceive it or comprehend it," which is beyond our mental capacities. I am neutral with respect to these competing interpretations. The point is that there are interpretations of Cartesian weak dialetheism that can significantly soften the metaphysical consequences of accepting possibly true theological dialetheia. Instead of locating any contradiction *in God* or his power, we can locate it *in ourselves*, in our language about him or in our finite minds; which is theologically unobjectionable: "Indeed, these are but the fringes of His ways; how faint is the whisper we hear of Him! Who then can understand the thunder of His power?" (Job 26:14).

Creeping Contradictions

Alternatively, a critic might instead complain that Cartesianism is logically untenable. Cartesianism claims to only entail possibly true dialetheia, but it would seem to entail actually true contradictions, too. Put another way, weak dialetheism entails strong dialetheism. Consequently, Cartesianism collapses into Cusanism. The objection is noteworthy but ultimately unconvincing. It reasons that, if one accepts that it is possible that a contradiction (e.g., $(p \land \sim p)$) obtains, then one must also accept that it is actually the case that a contradiction obtains – namely, the contradiction that it is both possible and impossible that the contradiction obtains.

$$\Diamond(p \land \sim p) \vdash \Diamond(p \land \sim p) \land \sim\Diamond(p \land \sim p)$$

Cotnoir (2017: sect. 3.2) offers a criticism of this type. It would seem to be especially troubling, since this inference is supposed to follow specifically from dialetheic modal logics, similar to what I have developed here (cf. Restall 1997; Priest 2008b). To demonstrate that this is the case, Cotnoir (2017: n. 14 – translated into my symbolism) writes:

> Assume that $v(\langle \blacklozenge(p \land \sim p), w \rangle)$ is designated; so $v(\langle(p \land \sim p), w^* \rangle)$ is designated too, which can only happen if $v(\langle(p \land \sim p), w^* \rangle) = \frac{1}{2}$. So, $v(\langle \blacklozenge(p \land \sim p), w \rangle) = \frac{1}{2}$. But then $v(\langle \sim\blacklozenge(p \land \sim p), w \rangle) = \frac{1}{2}$ too. Hence, $v(\langle \blacklozenge(p \land \sim p) \land \sim\blacklozenge (p \land \sim p), w \rangle) = \frac{1}{2}$, which is designated.

This argument, however, fails to convince. The argument cites that it is valid in LP to infer from $\blacklozenge(p \wedge \sim p)$ to $(\blacklozenge(p \wedge \sim p) \wedge \sim\blacklozenge(p \wedge \sim p))$. But whether or not this is a valid inference form in LP is irrelevant, since the relevant logic in this situation is CL, given that we are evaluating this proposition in world w. LP holds in w*, but not in w, too. By citing LP, therefore, this argument shows only that, if it is assumed that an actual contradiction may obtain (i.e., that LP is the logic governing the actual world), then it follows that an actual contradiction may obtain; which is circular and proves nothing. This error presents itself clearly in the inference from $v(<(p \wedge \sim p), w^*>) = \frac{1}{2}$ to $v(<\blacklozenge(p \wedge \sim p), w>) = \frac{1}{2}$ in Cotnoir's demonstration. But $\frac{1}{2}$ is not even a value in w, let alone a designated one. We said, rather, that $v(<\blacklozenge(p \wedge \sim p), w>)$ is designated – which is to say, $v = 1$ – so long as $v(<(p \wedge \sim p), w^*>) = 1$ or $\frac{1}{2}$. But with this correction, it follows that $v(<\sim\blacklozenge(p \wedge \sim p), w>) = 0$. Hence, it follows that $v(<\blacklozenge(p \wedge \sim p) \wedge \sim\blacklozenge(p \wedge \sim p), w>) = 0$, too, which is undesignated.

Let's review and conclude. The Cartesian revision of classical logic faces two potential counterarguments. The first is theological and argues that Cartesianism is inconsistent with the classical theologian's commitment to not speaking of God in terms of contradictions. I found this objection wanting because there is in fact a tradition of speaking of God in riddles, enigmas, and paradoxes. Moreover, there are many varieties of dialetheism, and some are hardly theologically controversial. And the second objection is that accepting Cartesianism puts one on a slippery slope to Cusanism, which would mean not simply revising classical logic but rejecting it outright, which is unacceptable. I found this objection wanting because it misunderstands the theological modal logic being proposed here. I believe, however, that this second strategy of attack on Cartesianism is the most potentially troubling. My remarks on this subject should not end the dialectic, but only prompt the critical analytic theist to continue it. In particular, my Cartesian response still demands that, in at least one respect, God's power is still constrained by *some* logic, even if nonclassical. Some careful explanation is still owed on this point.

Note that Cartesianism is not susceptible to the same objections facing Thomism. The Cartesian can flatly deny that Mr. McEar is omnipotent, since McEar cannot do absolutely everything. Additionally, the Cartesian can respond to the new stone paradox by saying that, even if God were to create a second essentially omnipotent being, he could still win a tug-of-war against him. In that case, both God and Titan would win the war. This is contradictory, but that's no problem, since God's power permits him even to violate the laws of logic (cf. De Florio & Frigerio 2015: 316). Finally, we said that the Thomist solution, were it successful, would resolve not only the stone paradox but a host of other, type-B theological paradoxes, too. The Cartesian solution also possesses the virtue of theoretical scope. Can the omnibenevolent, omnipotent God sin? The Cartesian can reply that he can – but only in an impossible world. In such a circumstance, God both is and is not omnibenevolent, an acceptable contradiction in our weakly dialetheist modal logic. And so, despite being sometimes dismissed as either too naïve or too absurd to take seriously, the Cartesian solution to the stone paradox is in fact highly defensible. I conclude therefore that, in accordance with our maxim of minimum mutilation for paradox resolution, Cartesianism would seem to be superior to all three of its competitors: McTaggartism, Cusanism, and even Thomism. Could God create a stone so heavy that even he can't lift it? The analytic classical theist should answer that he could: In his unfathomable power, God can lift even the unliftable, if he wills.

References

Adams, Sarah. 2015. "A New Paradox of Omnipotence." *Philosophia* 43 (3): 759–785.

Adams, Sarah, and Jon Robson. 2020. "Analyzing Aseity." *Canadian Journal of Philosophy* 50 (2): 251–267.

Aeschylus. 467 BC/2006. "Seven Against Thebes." In *Aeschylus*, Volume 1, Reprint Edition. Translated by Herbert Weir Smyth. Cambridge, MA: Loeb Classical Library.

Ahsan, Abbas. 2022. "Islamic Mystical Dialetheism: Resolving the Paradox of God's Unknowability and Ineffability." *Philosophia* 50 (3): 925–964.

Alanen, Lilli. 1985. "Descartes, Duns Scotus, and Ockham on Omnipotence and Possibility." *Franciscan Studies* 45 (1): 157–188.

Alanen, Lilli. 1988. "Descartes, Omnipotence, and Kinds of Modality." In *Doing Philosophy Historically*. Edited by Peter H. Hare. Buffalo, NY: Prometheus Books. pp. 182–196.

Al-Ghazali, Abu Hamid. c. 1096/1965. *The Jerusalem Epistle*. In his *Al-Ghazali's Tract on Dogmatic Theology*. Translated by A. L. Tibawi. London: Luzac and Company.

Al-Ghazali, Abu Hamid. c. 1105/2016. *The Alchemy of Happiness*. Translated by John Murray. London: The Lost Library.

Anderson, Alan Ross, and Nuel D. Belnap. 1975. *Entailment: The Logic of Relevance and Necessity*, Volume 1. Princeton, NJ: Princeton University Press.

Anderson, C. Anthony. 1984. "Divine Omnipotence and Impossible Tasks: An Intensional Analysis." *International Journal for Philosophy of Religion* 15 (3): 109–124.

Anselm of Canterbury. 1076/1975. *Monologion*. In his *Anselm of Canterbury*, Volume 1. Translated and edited by Jasper Hopkins and Herbert Richardson. Lewiston, NY: Edwin Mellen Press.

Anselm of Canterbury. 1077/1975. *Proslogion*. In his *Anselm of Canterbury*, Volume 1. Translated and edited by Jasper Hopkins and Herbert Richardson. Lewiston, NY: Edwin Mellen Press.

Antony, Louise. 2018. "No Good Reason – Exploring the Problem of Evil." In *The Norton Introduction to Philosophy*, Second Edition. Edited by Gideon Rosen, Alex Byrne, Joshua Cohen, Elizabeth Harman, and Seana Shiffrin. New York: Norton.

Aquinas, Thomas. c. 1255/2014. *On the Principles of Nature*. Translated by Eleonore Stump and Stephen Chanderbhan. In his *The Hackett*

Aquinas: Basic Works. Edited by Jeffrey Hause and Robert Pasnau. Indianapolis, IN: Hackett.

Aquinas, Thomas. 1259. *Disputed Questions on Truth*. Translated by Robert W. Mulligan, James V. McGlynn, and Robert W. Schmidt. Available online at isodore.co/aquinas/.

Aquinas, Thomas. 1265. *Summa Contra Gentiles*. Translated by Anton C. Pegis. Available online at isodore.co/aquinas/.

Aquinas, Thomas. 1271. *Commentary on Aristotle's Physics*. Translated by Richard J. Blackwell, Richard J. Spath, W. Edmund Thirlkel, and Pierre H. Conway. Available online at isodore.co/aquinas/.

Aquinas, Thomas. 1272. *Commentary on Aristotle's Metaphysics*. Translated by John P. Rowan. Available online at isodore.co/aquinas/.

Aquinas, Thomas. 1274/1952. *Summa Theologica*, Volume 1. Translated by The Fathers of the English Dominican Province. New Haven, CT: William Benton.

Aristotle. c. 350 BC/1941a. *The Categories*. Translated by E. M. Edghill. In *The Basic Works of Aristotle*. Edited by Richard McKeon. New York: Random House.

Aristotle. c. 350 BC/1941b. *The Ethics*. Translated by William D. Ross. In *The Basic Works of Aristotle*. Edited by Richard McKeon. New York: Random House.

Aristotle. c. 350 BC/1941c. *The Physics*. Translated by Reginald P. Hardie and Richard K. Gaye. In *The Basic Works of Aristotle*. Edited by Richard McKeon. New York: Random House.

Aristotle. c. 350 BCa. *The Prior Analytics*. Translated by A. J. Jenkinson. Available online at classics.mit.edu.

Aristotle. c. 350 BCb. *The Topics*. Translated by William A. Pickard-Cambridge. Available online at classics.mit.edu.

Augustine of Hippo. c. 397/1961. *The Confessions*. Translated by R. S. Pine-Coffin. London: Penguin.

Averroes. c. 1150/1969. *The Incoherence of the Incoherence*. Translated by Simon Van Den Bergh. London: Luzac and Company.

Baddorf, Matthew. 2017. "Divine Simplicity, Aseity, and Sovereignty." *Sophia* 56 (3): 403–418.

Baillie, James, and Jason Hagen. 2008. "There Cannot be Two Omnipotent Beings." *International Journal for Philosophy of Religion* 64 (1): 21–33.

Barth, Karl. 1936/1949. *The Doctrine of the Word of God*, Volume 1, Part 1. Translated by G. T. Thomson. Edinburgh: T&T Clark.

Barwise, Jon, and John Etchemendy. 2002. *Language, Proof, and Logic*. Stanford, CA: CSLI Publications.

Bassford, Andrew Dennis. 2019. "A Response to Chisholm's Paradox." *Philosophical Studies* 177 (4): 1137–1155.

Bassford, Andrew Dennis. 2020. "Malebranche on Intelligible Extension." *Metaphysica* 21 (2): 199–221.

Bassford, Andrew Dennis. 2021a. "God's Place in Logical Space." *Journal of Analytic Theology* 9: 100–125.

Bassford, Andrew Dennis. 2021b. "Essence, Effluence, and Emanation: A Neo-Suarezian Analysis." *Studia Neoaristotelica* 18 (2): 139–186.

Bassford, Andrew Dennis. 2022. "Ought Implies Can or Could Have." *Review of Metaphysics* 75 (4): 779–807.

Bassford, Andrew D., and Christopher Daniel Dolson. forthcoming. "Counterfactual Similarity, Nomic Indiscernibility, and the Paradox of Quidditism." *Inquiry.*

Beall, Jc. 2011. "Dialetheists Against Pinocchio." *Analysis* 71 (4): 689–691.

Beall, Jc. 2017. "There is No Logical Negation: True, False, Both, and Neither." *Australasian Journal of Logic* 14 (1): Article 1.

Beall, Jc. 2019. "On Contradictory Christology: Preliminary Remarks, Notation and Terminology." *Journal of Analytic Theology* 7 (1): 434–439.

Beall, Jc. 2021. *The Contradictory Christ.* Oxford: Oxford University Press.

Beall, Jc, and Aaron J. Cotnoir. 2017. "God of the Gaps: A Neglected Reply to God's Stone Problem." *Analysis* 77 (4): 681–689.

Beall, Jc, and David Ripley. 2004. "Analetheism and Dialetheism." *Analysis* 64 (1): 30–35.

Beall, Jc, and Bas C. van Fraassen. 2003. *Possibilities and Paradox: An Introduction to Modal and Many-Valued Logic.* Oxford: Oxford University Press.

Bergmann, Merrie, James Moor, and Jack Nelson. 2014. *The Logic Book*, Sixth Edition. New York: McGraw-Hill.

Berto, Francesco, and Mark Jago. Fall 2018. "Impossible Worlds." In *The Stanford Encyclopedia of Philosophy.* Edited by Edward N. Zalta. Available online at plato.stanford.edu.

Bittle, Celestine N. 1937. *Logic: The Science of Correct Thinking.* Milwaukee, WI: Bruce Publishing.

Bittle, Celestine N. 1939. *Ontology: The Domain of Being.* Milwaukee, WI: Bruce Publishing.

Bittle, Celestine N. 1941. *Cosmology: From Aether to Cosmos.* Milwaukee, WI: Bruce Publishing.

Bittle, Celestine N. 1953. *Theodicy: God and His Creatures.* Milwaukee, WI: Bruce Publishing.

Blumenfeld, David. 1978. "On the Compossibility of the Divine Attributes." *Philosophical Studies* 34 (1): 91–103.

Boethius, Anicius. 524/1999. *The Consolation of Philosophy*. Translated by Victor Watts. London: Penguin.

Bonaventure. 1259/1978. *The Soul's Journey into God*. In his *Bonaventure*. Translated by Ewert Cousins. New York: Paulist Press.

Bonevac, Daniel. 2012. "Two Theories of Analogical Predication." *Oxford Studies in Philosophy of Religion* 4 (1): 20–42.

Brower, Jeffrey E. 2008. "Making Sense of Divine Simplicity." *Faith and Philosophy* 25 (1): 3–30.

Brower, Jeffrey E. 2011. "Simplicity and Aseity." In *The Oxford Handbook of Philosophical Theology*. Edited by Thomas P. Flint and Michael C. Rea. Oxford: Oxford University Press.

Buridan, Jean. C. 1335/1985. *The Treatise on Consequences*. In *Jean Buridan's Logic*. Translated by Peter King. Dordrecht: Reidel.

Buridan, Jean. C. 1335. *Quaestiones in Analytica Posteriora*. (Translator unknown.) Available online at logicmuseum.com.

Burrus, Virginia. 2013. "Nothing Is Not One: Revisiting the Ex Nihilo." *Modern Theology* 29 (2): 33–48.

Chaudhuri, Haridas. 1954. "The Concept of Brahman in Hindu Philosophy." *Philosophy East and West* 4 (1): 47–66.

Clark, David W. 1971. "Voluntarism and Rationalism in the Ethics of Ockham." *Franciscan Studies* 31: 72–87.

Clark, Errin D. 2017. "Thomas Aquinas on Logic, Being, and Power, and Contemporary Problems for Divine Omnipotence." *Sophia* 56 (2): 247–261.

Clement of Alexandria. c. 200. *The Stromata, or Miscellanies*. (Translator unknown.) Available online at earlychristianwritings.com.

Collier, Matthew James. 2019. "God's Necessity on Anselmian Theistic Genuine Modal Realism." *Sophia* 58 (3): 331–348.

Conee, Earl. 1991. "The Possibility of Power Beyond Possibility." *Philosophical Perspectives* 5: 447–473.

Cotnoir, Aaron J. 2015. "Nāgārjuna's Logic." In *The Moon Points Back*. Edited by Koji Tanaka, Yasuo Deguchi, Jay L. Garfield, and Graham Priest. Oxford: Oxford University Press.

Cotnoir, Aaron J. 2017. "Theism and Dialetheism." *Australasian Journal of Philosophy* 96 (3): 592–609.

Cotnoir, Aaron J. 2019. "On the Role of Logic in Analytic Theology: Exploring the Wider Context of Beall's Philosophy of Logic." *Journal of Analytic Theology* 7: 508–528.

Cowan, J. L. 1965. "The Paradox of Omnipotence." *Analysis* 25 (3): 102–108.

Cowan, J. L. 1974. "The Paradox of Omnipotence Revisited." *Canadian Journal of Philosophy* 3 (3): 435–445.

Craig, William Lane. 2011. "Divine Eternity." In *The Oxford Handbook of Philosophical Theology*. Edited by Thomas P. Flint and Michael C. Rea. Oxford: Oxford University Press.

Creel, Richard E. 1980. "Can God Know that He Is God?" *Religious Studies* 16 (2): 195–201.

Curley, Edward M. 1984. "Descartes on the Creation of the Eternal Truths." *Philosophical Review* 93 (4): 569–597.

Damian, Peter. 1065/1969. *On Divine Omnipotence*. Translated by Owen J. Blum. In *Medieval Philosophy: From St. Augustine to Nicholas of Cusa*. Edited by John F. Wippel and Allan B. Wolter. New York: The Free Press.

De Florio, Ciro, and Aldo Frigerio. 2015. "Two Omnipotent Beings?" *Philosophia* 43 (2): 309–324.

Descartes, René. 1629–1649/1970. *Philosophical Letters*. Translated by Anthony Kenny. Indianapolis, IN: Basil Blackwell.

Descartes, René. 1641/2006. *Meditations, Objections, and Replies*. Translated by Roger Ariew and Donald Cress. Cambridge, MA: Hackett.

Descartes, René. 1647/1996. *Principles of Philosophy*. In his *The Philosophical Writings of Descartes*, Volume 1. Translated by John Cottingham, Robert Stoothoff, and Dugald Murdoch. Cambridge: Cambridge University Press.

Descartes, René. 1677/1996. *The World*. In his *The Philosophical Writings of Descartes*, Volume 1. Translated by John Cottingham, Robert Stoothoff, and Dugald Murdoch. Cambridge: Cambridge University Press.

Devenish, Philip E. 1985. "Omnipotence, Creation, Perfection: Kenny and Aquinas on the Power and Action of God." *Modern Theology* 1 (2): 105–117.

Devlin, Keith. 1992. *Sets, Functions, and Logic: An Introduction to Abstract Mathematics*, Second Edition. New York: Chapman & Hall.

Drange, Theodore M. 2003. "Gale on Omnipotence." *Philo* 6 (1): 23–26.

Englebretsen, George. 1971. "The Incompatibility of God's Existence and Omnipotence." *Sophia* 10 (1): 28–31.

Evans, C. Stephen. 2008. "Kierkegaard and the Limits of Reason: Can There Be a Responsible Fideism?" *Revista Portuguesa de Filosofia* 64 (4): 1021–1035.

Evans, Gillian R. 1994. *Philosophy and Theology in the Middle Ages*. New York: Routledge.

Fine, Kit. 1970. "Propositional Quantifiers in Modal Logic." *Theoria* 36 (3): 336–346.

Fine, Kit. 1994. "Essence and Modality." *Philosophical Perspectives* 8: 1–16.

Fine, Kit. 2010. "Some Puzzles of Ground." *Notre Dame Journal of Formal Logic* 51 (1): 97–118.

Flint, Thomas P. 1983. "The Problem of Divine Freedom." *American Philosophical Quarterly* 20 (3): 255–264.

Flint, Thomas P. 1998. "Divine Providence." In *The Oxford Handbook of Philosophical Theology*. Edited by Thomas P. Flint and Michael C. Rea. Oxford: Oxford University Press.

Flint, Thomas P., and Alfred J. Freddoso. 1983. "Maximal Power." In *The Existence and Nature of God*. Edited by Alfred J. Freddoso. Notre Dame, IN: University of Notre Dame Press.

Frankfurt, Harry. 1964. "The Logic of Omnipotence." *Philosophical Review* 73 (2): 262–263.

Frankfurt, Harry. 1969. "Alternative Possibilities and Moral Responsibility." *Journal of Philosophy* 66 (23): 829–839.

Frankfurt, Harry. 1977. "Descartes on the Creation of the Eternal Truths." *Philosophical Review* 86 (1): 36–57.

Fujii, John N. 1961/1963. *An Introduction to the Elements of Mathematics*. New York: John Wiley & Sons.

Gaon, Saadia. 933/1984. *The Book of Beliefs and Opinions*. Translated by Samuel Rosenblatt. New Haven, CT: Yale University Press.

Geach, Peter T. 1973. "Omnipotence." *Philosophy* 48 (183): 7–20.

Goldfarb, Warren. 2003. *Deductive Logic*. Indianapolis, IN: Hackett.

Grim, Patrick. 1983. "Some Neglected Problems of Omniscience." *American Philosophical Quarterly* 20 (3): 265–276.

Grim, Patrick. 1984. "There is No Set of All Truths." *Analysis* 44 (4): 206–208.

Grim, Patrick. 1990. "On Omniscience and a 'Set of All Truths': A Reply to Bringsjord." *Analysis* 50 (4): 271–276.

Grim, Patrick. 2000. "The Being That Knew Too Much." *International Journal for Philosophy of Religion* 47 (3): 141–154.

Hallman, Joseph M. 1999. "Can God Suffer?" *Logos* 2 (1): 153–175.

Hasker, William. 1989. *God, Time, and Knowledge*. Ithaca, NY: Cornell University Press.

Heck, Richard Kimberly. 2012. "Solving Frege's Puzzle." *Journal of Philosophy* 109: 132–174.

Hick, John. 1963. *Philosophy of Religion*, Third Edition. London: Prentice Hall.

Hill, Daniel. 1998. "What's New in Philosophy of Religion?" *Philosophical Now* 21: 30–33.

Hill, Scott. 2014. "Giving Up Omnipotence." *Canadian Journal of Philosophy* 44 (1): 97–117.

Holopainen, Toivo J. 2020. "Peter Damian." In *The Stanford Encyclopedia of Philosophy*. Edited by Edward N. Zalta. Available online at plato.stanford.edu.

Hu, Shih. 1922/1963. *The Development of the Logical Method in Ancient China*. New York: Arno Press.

Huggett, Nick. 2019. "Zeno's Paradoxes." In *The Stanford Encyclopedia of Philosophy*. Edited by Edward N. Zalta. Available online at plato .stanford.edu.

Hunt, David, and Linda Zagzebski. 2022. "Foreknowledge and Free Will." In *The Stanford Encyclopedia of Philosophy*. Edited by Edward N. Zalta. Available online at plato.stanford.edu.

Juster, Norton. 1961. *The Phantom Tollbooth*. New York: Scholastic.

Kaufman, Dan. 2002. "Descartes's Creation Doctrine and Modality." *Australasian Journal of Philosophy* 80 (1): 24–41.

Keas, Michael N. 2018. "Systematizing the Theoretical Virtues." *Synthese* 195 (6): 2761–2793.

Kelley, David. 1998. *The Art of Reasoning*, Third Edition. New York: Norton.

Kenny, Anthony. 1979. *The God of the Philosophers*. Oxford: Clarendon Press.

Kleene, Stephen Cole. 1952. *Introduction to Metamathematics*. Amsterdam: North-Holland Publishers.

Knepper, Timothy D. 2008. "Not Not: The Method and Logic of Dionysian Negation." *American Catholic Philosophical Quarterly* 82 (4): 619–637.

Koistinen, Olli. 2003. "Spinoza's Proof of Necessitarianism." *Philosophy and Phenomenological Research* 67 (2): 283–310.

Koons, Robert C. 2014. "A New Kalam Argument: Revenge of the Grim Reaper." *Nous* 48 (2): 256–267.

Kripke, Saul A. 1959. "A Completeness Theorem in Modal Logic." *Journal of Symbolic Logic* 24 (1): 1–14.

Kripke, Saul A. 1963a. "Semantical Considerations on Modal Logic." *Acta Philosophica Fennica* 16: 83–94.

Kripke, Saul A. 1963b. "Semantical Analysis of Modal Logic I: Normal Propositional Calculi." *Zeitschrift fur Mathematische Logik und Grundlagen der Mathematik* 9: 67–96.

Kripke, Saul A. 1965. "Semantical Analysis of Modal Logic II: Non-Normal Modal Propositional Calculi." In *The Theory of Models: Proceedings of the 1963 International Symposium at Berkeley*. Edited by John W. Addison, Alfred Tarski, and Leon Henkin. Amsterdam: North-Holland Publishers.

La Croix, Richard R. 1975. "Swinburne on Omnipotence." *International Journal for Philosophy of Religion* 6 (4): 251–255.

La Croix, Richard R. 1977. "The Impossibility of Defining Omnipotence." *Philosophical Studies* 32 (2): 181–190.

La Croix, Richard R. 1984. "Descartes on God's Ability to Do the Logically Impossible." *Canadian Journal of Philosophy* 14 (3): 455–475.

Lactanitius. c. 300/1871. *On the Wrath of God*. In his *The Works of Lactanitius*. Translated by William Fletcher. Edinburgh: T&T Clark.

Lagerlund, Henrik. Summer 2022. "Medieval Theories of the Syllogism." In *The Stanford Encyclopedia of Philosophy*. Edited by Edward N. Zalta. Available online at plato.stanford.edu.

Laughlin, Peter. 2009. "Divine Necessity and Created Contingence in Aquinas." *Heythrop Journal* 50 (4): 648–657.

Leftow, Brian. 2011. "Omnipotence." In *The Oxford Handbook of Philosophical Theology*. Edited by Thomas P. Flint and Michael C. Rea. Oxford: Oxford University Press.

Leftow, Brian. 2012. "God's Omnipotence." In *The Oxford Handbook of Aquinas*. Edited by Brian Davies. Oxford: Oxford University Press.

Lemmon, E. J. 1965/1969. *Beginning Logic*. London: Nelson.

Lewis, Clive S. 1940/1962. *The Problem of Pain*. New York: Macmillan.

Lewis, Clarence Irving, and Cooper Harold Langford. 1932. *Symbolic Logic*. New York: The Century Company.

Lewis, David K. 1973/2005. *Counterfactuals*. Malden, MA: Blackwell.

Lewis, David K. 1978. "Truth in Fiction." *American Philosophical Quarterly* 15 (1): 37–46.

Lewis, David K. 1979. "Counterfactual Dependence and Time's Arrow." *Nous* 13 (4): 455–476.

Lewis, David K. 1986/2005. *On the Plurality of Worlds*. Malden, MA: Blackwell.

Linksy, Bernard. 1999. *Russell's Metaphysical Logic*. Stanford, CA: CSLI Publications.

Lombard, Peter. c. 1155/2007. *The Sentences*, Book 1. Translated by Giulio Silano. Toronto: Pontifical Institute of Medieval Studies.

Londey, David, Barry Miller, and John King-Farlow. 1971. "God and the Stone Paradox: Three Comments." *Sophia* 10 (3): 23–33.

Mackie, John L. 1955. "Evil and Omnipotence." *Mind* 64 (254): 200–212.

Macquarrie, John. 1967. *God-Talk: An Examination of the Language and Logic of Theology*. New York: Harper & Row.

Maimonides, Moses. 1190/1956. *The Guide for the Perplexed*. Translated by Moses Friedlander. New York: Dover.

Malebranche, Nicolas. 1678/1997. *Elucidations of The Search after Truth*. Translated by Thomas M. Lennon. In his *The Search after Truth*. Edited by Thomas M. Lennon and Paul J. Olscamp. Cambridge: Cambridge University Press.

Malebranche, Nicolas. 1688/1997. *Dialogues on Metaphysics and on Religion*. Translated by David Scott. Edited by Nicholas Jolley. Cambridge: Cambridge University Press.

Mallozzi, Antonella, Anand Vaidya, and Michael Wallner. 2021. "The Epistemology of Modality." In *The Stanford Encyclopedia of Philosophy*. Edited by Edward N. Zalta. Available online at plato.stanford.edu.

Mares, Edwin D. 2004. "Semantic Dialetheism." In *The Law of Non-Contradiction*. Edited by Graham Priest, Jc Beall, and Bradley Armour-Garb. Oxford: Clarendon.

Mavrodes, George. 1963. "Some Puzzles Concerning Omnipotence." *Philosophical Review* 72 (2): 221–223.

Mavrodes, George. 1977. "Defining Omnipotence." *Philosophical Studies* 32 (2): 191–202.

Mavrodes, George. 1988. "Commentary on Lilli Alanen's 'Descartes, Omnipotence, and Kinds of Modality.'" In *Doing Philosophy Historically*. Edited by Peter H. Hare. Buffalo, NY: Prometheus Books. pp. 197–202.

Mayo, Bernard. 1961. "Mr. Keene on Omnipotence." *Mind* 70 (278): 249–250.

McDaniel, Kris. 2020. "John M. E. McTaggart." In *The Stanford Encyclopedia of Philosophy*. Edited by Edward N. Zalta. Available online at plato .stanford.edu.

McFetridge, Ian G. 1990. "Descartes on Modality." In his *Logical Necessity and Other Essays*. Bristol: Longdunn Press.

McTaggart, John M. E. 1906. *Some Dogmas of Religion*. London: Edward Arnold Publisher.

Mele, Alfred R., and M. P. Smith. 1988. "The New Paradox of the Stone." *Faith and Philosophy* 5 (3): 283–290.

Miller, Clyde Lee. 2021. "Nicholas of Cusa." In *The Stanford Encyclopedia of Philosophy*. Edited by Edward N. Zalta. Available online at plato .stanford.edu.

Molina, Luis de. 1588/1988. *On Divine Foreknowledge (Part IV of the* Concordia*)*. Translated by Alfred J. Freddoso. Ithaca, NY: Cornell University Press.

Moody, Ernest A. 1966/1975. "The Medieval Contribution to Logic." In his *Studies in Medieval Philosophy, Science, and Logic: Collected* Papers, *1933–1969*. Berkley: University of California Press.

Morris, Thomas V. 1991. *Our Idea of God*. Notre Dame, IN: University of Notre Dame Press.

Morriston, Wes. 2001. "Omnipotence and the Anselmian God." *Philo* 4 (1): 7–20.

Morriston, Wes. 2002. "Omnipotence and the Power to Choose: A Reply to Wielenberg." *Faith and Philosophy* 19 (3): 358–367.

Nagasawa, Yujin. 2008. "A New Defense of Anselmian Theism." *Philosophical Quarterly* 58 (233): 577–596.

Nicholas of Cusa. 1440/1969. *On Learned Ignorance*, Chapters 2–3. Translated by G. Heron. In *Medieval Philosophy: From St. Augustine to Nicholas of Cusa*. Edited by John F. Wippel and Allan B. Wolter. New York: The Free Press.

Nolan, Daniel. 2021. "Impossibility and Impossible Worlds." In *The Routledge Handbook of Modality*. Edited by Otavio Bueno and Scott Shalkowski. New York: Routledge.

Northrop, Forrest S. C. 1947/1983. *The Logic of the Sciences and the Humanities*. Woodbridge, CT: Ox Bow Press.

Oms, Sergi. forthcoming. "Some Remarks on the Notion of Paradox." *Acta Analytica*.

Origen of Alexandria. c. 230/1966. *On First Principles*. Translated by G. W. Butterworth. New York: Harper.

Pearce, Kenneth L. 2017. "Counterpossible Dependence and the Efficacy of the Divine Will." *Faith and Philosophy* 34 (1): 3–16.

Pearce, Kenneth L. 2019. "Infinite Power and Finite Powers." In *The Infinity of God: New Perspectives in Theology and Philosophy*. Edited by Benedikt Paul Goecke and Christian Tapp. Notre Dame, IN: Notre Dame University Press.

Pearce, Kenneth L. 2021. "God's Impossible Options." *Faith and Philosophy* 38 (2): 185–204.

Pearce, Kenneth L., and Alexander R. Pruss. 2012. "Understanding Omnipotence." *Religious Studies* 48 (3): 403–414.

Pike, Nelson. 1969. "Omnipotence and God's Ability to Sin." *American Philosophical Quarterly* 6 (3): 208–216.

Pojman, Louis P. 2003. "The Problem of Evil." In his *Philosophy of Religion: An Anthology*, Fourth Edition. Edited by Louis P. Pojman. Toronto: Wadsworth.

Porro, Pasquale. 2014. "Henry of Ghent." In *The Stanford Encyclopedia of Philosophy*. Edited by Edward N. Zalta. Available online at plato.stanford.edu.

Plantinga, Alvin. 1967/1994. *God and Other Minds: A Study of the Rational Justification of Belief in God*. Ithaca, NY: Cornell University Press.

Plantinga, Alvin. 1970. "World and Essence." *Philosophical Review* 79 (4): 461–492.

Plantinga, Alvin. 1974. *The Nature of Necessity*. Oxford: Clarendon Press.

Plantinga, Alvin. 1977. *God, Freedom, and Evil*. Grand Rapids, MI: Eerdmans Publishing.

Plantinga, Alvin. 1979/1983/2003. "Religious Belief Without Evidence." In *Philosophy of Religion: An Anthology*, Fourth Edition. Edited by Louis P. Pojman. Toronto: Wadsworth.

Plantinga, Alvin. 1980. *Does God Have a Nature?* Milwaukee, WI: Marquette University Press.

Plantinga, Alvin, and Patrick Grim. 1993. "Truth, Omniscience, and Cantorian Arguments: An Exchange." *Philosophical Studies* 71 (3): 267–306.

Plotinus. c. 253/1952. *The Six Enneads*. Translated by Stephen MacKenna and B. S. Page. London: William Benton.

Priest, Graham. 1979. "The Logic of Paradox." *Journal of Philosophical Logic* 8 (1): 219–241.

Priest, Graham. 1987. *In Contradiction: A Study of the Transconsistent*. Dordrecht: Martinus Nijhoff Publishers.

Priest, Graham. 1992. "What is a Non-Normal World?" *Logique et Analyse* 35 (140): 291–302.

Priest, Graham. 2008a. *An Introduction to Non-Classical Logic: From If to Is*, Second Edition. Cambridge: Cambridge University Press.

Priest, Graham. 2008b. "Many-Valued Modal Logics: A Simple Approach." *Review of Symbolic Logic* 1 (2): 190–203.

Priest, Graham, Francesco Berto, and Zach Weber. 2018. "Dialetheism." In *The Stanford Encyclopedia of Philosophy*. Edited by Edward N. Zalta. Available online at plato.stanford.edu.

Priest, Graham, Koji Tanaka, and Zach Weber. 2022. "Paraconsistent Logic." In *The Stanford Encyclopedia of Philosophy*. Edited by Edward N. Zalta. Available online at plato.stanford.edu.

Prior, Arthur N. 1955. "Diodoran Modalities." *Philosophical Quarterly* 5 (20): 205–213.

Pruss, Alexander R., and Joshua L. Rasmussen. 2018. *Necessary Existence*. Oxford: Oxford University Press.

Pseudo-Dionysius the Areopagite. c. 500/1897. *Divine Names*. In his *The Works of Dionysius the Areopagite*, Volume 1. Translated by John Parker. London: James Parker and Company.

Pseudo-Grosseteste. c. 1277/1957. *Summa Philosophiae*, Treatises 2–3. In *Selections from Medieval Philosophers*, Volume 1. Edited and translated by Richard McKeon. New York: Scribner.

Quine, William V. O. 1947. "The Problem of Interpreting Modal Logic." *Journal of Symbolic Logic* 12 (2): 42–48.

Quine, William V. O. 1951/2003. "Two Dogmas of Empiricism." In his *From a Logical Point of View: Nine Logico-Philosophical Essays*. Cambridge, MA: Harvard University Press.

Quine, William V. O. 1961/1966. "The Ways of Paradox." In his *The Ways of Paradox and Other Essays*. New York: Random House.

Quine, William V. O. 1986. *Philosophy of Logic*, Second Edition. Cambridge, MA: Harvard University Press.

Quine, W. V. O., and J. S. Ullian. 1970. *The Web of Belief*. New York: Random House.

Rehnman, Sebastian. 2008. "Does It Matter If Christian Doctrine Is Contradictory? Barth on Logic and Theology." In *Engaging with Barth: Contemporary Evangelical Critiques*. Edited by David Gibson and Daniel Strange. Edinburgh: T&T Clark.

Remnant, Peter. 1978. "Peter Damian: Could God Change the Past?" *Canadian Journal of Philosophy* 8 (2): 259–268.

Restall, Greg. 1997. "Paraconsistent Logics!" *Bulletin of the Section of Logic* 26 (3): 156–163.

Rosenkrantz, Gary, and Joshua Hoffman. 1980. "What an Omnipotent Agent Can Do." *International Journal for Philosophy of Religion* 11 (1): 1–19.

Rosenkrantz, Gary, and Joshua Hoffman. 1988. "Omnipotence Redux." *Philosophy and Phenomenological Research* 49 (2): 283–301.

Rosenkrantz, Gary, and Joshua Hoffman. 2022. "Omnipotence." In *The Stanford Encyclopedia of Philosophy*. Edited by Edward N. Zalta. Available online at plato.stanford.edu.

Rowe, William L. 2002. "Can God Be Free?" *Faith and Philosophy* 19 (4): 405–424.

Russell, Bertrand. 1903/1965. Principles of Mathematics, Second Edition. New York: Norton.

Russell, Bertrand. 1905. "On Denoting." *Mind* 14 (56): 479–493.

Sainsbury, Richard M. 2008. *Paradoxes*. Cambridge: Cambridge University Press.

Sandgren, Alexander, and Koji Tanaka. 2020. "Two Kinds of Logical Impossibility." *Nous* 54 (4): 795–806.

Savage, Curtis Wade. 1967. "The Paradox of the Stone." *Philosophical Review* 76 (1): 74–79.

Schrader, David E. 1979. "A Solution to the Stone Paradox." *Synthese* 42 (2): 255–264.

Scotus, John Duns. c. 1300/1987. "The Unicity of God." In his *Philosophical Writings: A Selection*, Second Edition. Translated by Allan Wolter. Indianapolis, IN: Hackett.

Serway, Raymond A., and Chris Vuille. 2015. *College Physics*, Tenth Edition. Boston, MA: Cengage Learning.

Sider, Theodore. 2010. *Logic for Philosophy*. Oxford: Oxford University Press.

Sobel, Jordan Howard. 2004. *Logic and Theism: Arguments for and Against Beliefs in God*. Cambridge: Cambridge University Press.

Sorensen, Roy. 2005. *A Brief History of the Paradox: Philosophy and the Labyrinths of the Mind*. Oxford: Oxford University Press.

Spinoza, Baruch. 1677/2005. *Ethics and On the Improvement of the Understanding*. Translated by Robert H. M. Elwes. New York: Barnes and Noble.

Starr, William. 2021. "Counterfactuals." In *The Stanford Encyclopedia of Philosophy*. Edited by Edward N. Zalta. Available online at plato .stanford.edu.

Stump, Eleanore. 1985. "The Problem of Evil." *Faith and Philosophy* 2 (4): 392–423.

Suárez, Francisco. 1597/1983. *Metaphysical Disputations*, Disputation 31. In his *On the Essence of Finite Being as Such, on the Essence of That Essence and Their Distinction*. Translated by Norman J. Wells. Milwaukee, WI: Marquette University Press.

Suzuki, Daisetsu T. 1934. *An Introduction to Zen Buddhism*. New York: Grove Press.

Swanson, Eric. 2008. "Modality in Language." *Philosophy Compass* 3 (6): 1193–1207.

Świętorzecka, Kordula. 2011. "Some Remarks on Formal Description of God's Omnipotence." *Logic and Logical Philosophy* 20 (4): 307–315.

Swinburne, Richard. 1973. "Omnipotence." *American Philosophical Quarterly* 10 (3): 231–237.

Swinburne, Richard. 1994. *The Christian God*. Oxford: Oxford University Press.

Talbott, Thomas B. 1988. "On the Divine Nature and the Nature of Divine Freedom." *Faith and Philosophy* 5 (1): 3–24.

Tanaka, Koji. 2018. "Logically Impossible Worlds." *Australasian Journal of Logic* 15 (2): 489–497.

Tedder, Andrew. 2020. "A Classical Bimodal Logic with Varying Essences." In *The Logica Yearbook 2019*. Edited by Igor Sedlár and Martin Blicha. Prague: College Publications.

Tedder, Andrew, and Guillermo Badia. 2018. "Currying Omnipotence: A Reply to Beall and Cotnoir." *Thought* 7 (2): 119–121.

Thai, Lee Pham, and Jerry Pillay. 2020. "Can God Create Humans with Free Will who Never Commit Evil?" *HTS Theological Studies* 76 (1): A6102.

Thomason, Richmond H. 1980. "A Model Theory for Propositional Attitudes." *Linguistics and Philosophy* 4: 47–70.

Tillemans, Tom J. F. 1999. *Scripture, Logic, Language: Essays on Dharmakīrti and His Tibetan Successors*. Somerville, MA: Wisdom Publications.

Trakakis, Nick. 1997. "The Absolutist Theory of Omnipotence." *Sophia* 36 (2): 55–78.

Uckelman, Sara L. 2009. *Modalities in Medieval Logic*. PhD Thesis, University of Amsterdam.

Uzquiano, Gabriel. 2020. "Quantifiers and Quantification." In *The Stanford Encyclopedia of Philosophy*. Edited by Edward N. Zalta. Available online at plato.stanford.edu.

Vaughn, Lewis. 2016. *The Power of Critical Thinking: Effective Reasoning about Ordinary and Extraordinary Claims*, Fifth Edition. Oxford: Oxford University Press.

Werner, Louis. 1971. "Some Omnipotent Beings!" *Critica* 5 (14): 55–72.

Wertz, S. K. 1984. "Descartes and the Paradox of the Stone." *Sophia* 23 (1): 16–24.

Wielenberg, Erik J. 2000. "Omnipotence Again." *Faith and Philosophy* 17 (1): 26–47.

Wielenberg, Erik J. 2001. "The New Paradox of the Stone Revisited." *Faith and Philosophy* 18 (2): 261–268.

Wierenga, Edward. 1983. "Omnipotence Defined." *Philosophy and Phenomenological Research* 43 (3): 363–375.

Wierenga, Edward. 1989. *The Nature of God*. Ithaca, NY: Cornell University Press.

William of Ockham. 1318/1979. *Commentary on the Sentences of Peter Lombard* (*Ordinatio*, Distinctions 19–48). In his *Opera Theologica*, Volume 4. Translated by Gedeon Gál and Stephen F. Brown. Edited by Gerald Etzkorn and Francis Kelly. St. Bonaventure: The Franciscan Institute.

Wittgenstein, Ludwig. 1922/2003. *Tractatus Logico-Philosophicus*. Translated by Charles K. Ogden. New York: Barnes & Noble.

Wittgenstein, Ludwig. 1938/1966. "A Lecture on Religious Belief." In his *Lectures and Conversations on Aesthetics, Psychology, and Religious Belief*. Edited by Cyril Barrett. Berkeley: University of California Press.

Yagisawa, Takashi. 1988. "Beyond Possible Worlds." *Philosophical Studies* 53 (2): 175–204.

Yagisawa, Takashi. 1992. "Possible Worlds as Shifting Domains." *Erkenntnis* 36 (1): 83–101.

Yagisawa, Takashi. 2010. *Worlds and Individuals, Possible and Otherwise*. Oxford: Oxford University Press.

Yagisawa, Takashi. 2015. "Impossibilia and Modally Tensed Predication." *Acta Analytica* 30 (4): 317–323.

Young, Robert. 1976. "Omnipotence and Compatibilism." *Philosophia* 6 (1): 49–67.

Acknowledgments

I would like to express thanks to my friends and colleagues, Ron Avni, Dan Bonevac, Sam Cantor, Henry Curtis, Josh Dever, Jim Hankinson, Jon Litland, Ross Preuss Greene, and my anonymous reviewers; special thanks to Rob Koons. Without their help, completing this Element would have been a burden too heavy to bear.

Cambridge Elements ≡

The Problems of God

Series Editor

Michael L. Peterson

Asbury Theological Seminary

Michael Peterson is Professor of Philosophy at Asbury Theological Seminary. He is the author of *God and Evil* (Routledge); *Monotheism, Suffering, and Evil* (Cambridge University Press); *With All Your Mind* (University of Notre Dame Press); *C. S. Lewis and the Christian Worldview* (Oxford University Press); *Evil and the Christian God* (Baker Book House); and *Philosophy of Education: Issues and Options* (Intervarsity Press). He is co-author of *Reason and Religious Belief* (Oxford University Press); *Science, Evolution, and Religion: A Debate about Atheism and Theism* (Oxford University Press); and *Biology, Religion, and Philosophy* (Cambridge University Press). He is editor of *The Problem of Evil: Selected Readings* (University of Notre Dame Press). He is co-editor of *Philosophy of Religion: Selected Readings* (Oxford University Press) and *Contemporary Debates in Philosophy of Religion* (Wiley-Blackwell). He served as General Editor of the Blackwell monograph series Exploring Philosophy of Religion and is founding Managing Editor of the journal *Faith and Philosophy*.

About the Series

This series explores problems related to God, such as the human quest for God or gods, contemplation of God, and critique and rejection of God. Concise, authoritative volumes in this series will reflect the methods of a variety of disciplines, including philosophy of religion, theology, religious studies, and sociology.

Cambridge Elements ☰

The Problems of God

Elements in the Series

A full series listing is available at: www.cambridge.org/EPOG